MW01068807

Syracuse

Syracuse

Sicily's City of Stories

Joachim Sartorius

Translated by Stephen Brown

First English edition published in Great Britain in 2024 by
Haus Publishing
4 Cinnamon Row
London SW11 3TW

Copyright © 2023 by mareverlag, Hamburg
Copyright of the English translation © Stephen Brown, 2024

First published in German as *Die Versuchung von Syrakus*

The moral right of the authors have been asserted

A CIP catalogue record for this book is available
from the British Library

ISBN: 978-1-914982-12-5
eISBN: 978-1-914982-13-2

Typeset in Garamond by MacGuru Ltd
Printed in the UK by TJ Books

For Karin

'But for me there may be something even
lovelier to come in Syracuse.'

Sigmund Freud to Martha Freud,
in a letter from Palermo dated 18 September 1910

Contents

Being There

1.

Giuseppe Monteleone had been a police officer in Syracuse for thirty-eight years. He'd retired over ten years ago but he was an imposing figure still, in spite of his paunch and, lately, the heaviness in his legs. His most striking feature was his head, which closely resembled that of Emperor Vespasian: a sharp nose, chiselled jaw, close-cropped white sideburns, bulging neck, and nimble, flashing eyes. He lived in Ortigia, in a roomy apartment on Piazza del Precursore next to the deconsecrated gothic church of San Giovanni Battista, with a black and white dog, a mongrel mix of pinscher and miniature terrier, which yapped constantly in falsetto and thought that I, who lived in the building opposite, just two storeys higher up, was not its friend. Piazza del Precursore is in the Giudecca, the old Jewish quarter. The Giudecca is part of Ortigia and Ortigia itself is an island, the 'quail island', and the oldest part of the large and once mighty city of Syracuse.

When I bought my apartment on Piazza del Precursore – I liked it above all for its large terrace with a view of the open sea and the brisk traffic of ships – I got to know four people almost simultaneously: my neighbour, Giuseppe Monteleone; the translator Dora Suma, who helped me with all the documents I had to have notarised; the painter Gaetano Tranchino; and Baron Lucio Tasca di Lignari, scion of the old Sicilian nobility, whose massy weariness reminded me at our first meeting of the prince in Lampedusa's famous novel, *The Leopard*, and who lived in one of the palaces that line Piazza Duomo.

Why Syracuse? Why Ortigia? When my mother died, I suddenly had some money. Unimaginative as I am in financial matters, I thought I ought to invest it in property, preferably at the southern end of Europe, preferably on or in the Mediterranean. Sicily came to mind. I'd already visited the island several times before and liked it immediately, even the things that people generally like least – the motorways, for instance, which in early summer were so thickly bordered with oleander and the frothing crimson of bougainvillea that you might think you were in some endless tracking shot through a sea of blossom. I liked North-African-ish Trapani, the island of Mozia, the great heap of ruins that is Selinunte, the Greek temples at Agrigento, at sight of which even the dumbest has to think 'sublime', and the harsh landscape of the interior, of Enna and Caltagirone. But it was Syracuse that stayed with me most strongly. I had once – it might have been more than twenty years earlier – walked all the way round Ortigia. It takes no more than fifty minutes. You could sense the vastness of the sea everywhere. It shimmered at the end of every street. The light made Ortigia all at once a city of white. And straightaway I felt this as well: on this small island, memories and remnants of events that had taken place decades and centuries and millennia ago were layered on top of each other. How such an island dealt with its past and with its decline, for it had been a great past, interested me very much.

2.

I try to imagine those first Greek settlers, who came from Corinth and skimmed the east coast of Sicily searching for the ideal spot to colonise and establish a maritime base. They sailed along the coast, starting, most likely, from what today is Augusta. It takes a breakneck imagination to picture that stretch of land, now overrun by oil refineries and hideously built up, in its untouched state – only broom and maquis and conifers and colonies of bees. The Corinthians discovered a small bay, then a slender island, poking out into the Ionian Sea, and then a large bay hemmed in by the peninsula known in the time of Virgil as Plemyrium and today as Plemmirio. They must have struggled to contain their excitement. Twin natural harbours, one of which is always protected no matter which way the storm winds are blowing, are a rare find and a harbour as large as Porto Grande would have been beyond their dreams. In 734 BC, if we believe the historians, they founded their first settlement here, ancient Syrakusai. Four hundred years later Syracuse was a cosmopolitan city, which had cut the Carthaginians down to size and was challenging Athens for its status as first city of the Mediterranean.

3.

There are evenings, today, when Ortigia lies in a sea of the imagination. Look precisely and your eye detects the lines behind the bastions and the houses, and the walls open out this old world like a fan.

4.

Monteleone stands on his balcony in his dressing gown with its worn cords. In spite of the withered dwarf cacti at his feet, in spite of the scruffy narrowness of the balcony, he is an emperor. Didn't the old tyrants of Syracuse – Gelon, Hieron, Dionysius, and Dion – look exactly like this?

In history the figures that fascinate us the most are those about whose lives we have only a few secure facts. We gather fragments from Diodorus or Herodotus and little by little something almost like a real person emerges. But it is the legends woven around these figures that form much the greater and more defining element. From this compound of fact and fantasy a mythical being emerges, something almost like a demigod. After I read my first books on the history of Syracuse, Dionysius I became for me just such a semi-divine being, the most impressive figure among all the impressive tyrants of Syracuse.

At just twenty-five years old, he must have exploded onto the political scene like a supernova. The cities that were not allied with Syracuse he subjugated, or razed to the ground. He built up the island of Ortigia, the oldest part of Syracuse, into a single, heavily fortified palace. He circled the new town with a wall twenty-seven kilometres in length, a crazily gigantic structure. In hard-fought battles, he drove the Carthaginians, who occupied almost all of Sicily at the beginning of the fifth century BC, back into the western part of the island. A man who had annexed all of Calabria and parts of the Balkans by the time of his death, whose only rival in power was the king of Persia himself, must have been an entirely cunning, power-crazed, brutal person. Yet his biographers tell stories of his tenderness too, his artist's soul. They say that he loved the theatre and had a *cavea* built, the forerunner of the great Greek theatre, which was completed under Hieron II in 220 BC and could hold an audience of 15,000. They say he so admired Euripides that he bought the writing tablets, writing instruments, and zither used by the great tragedian and then laid them as offerings in a 'Temple of the Muses' on Ortigia, in a specially crafted shrine, which he visited in lulls between campaigns.

Does Giuseppe Monteleone know, as he hoists up a basket on a string, into which a neighbour has put a pale loaf of bread and a bottle of milk, does he know he looks so much like Dionysius I, in my imagination at least? I will ask him next time we chat whether it is true what one Syracusan is supposed to have said once to his ruler: 'Oh Dionysius! Tyranny is a beautiful funeral shroud.' Like his predecessor, the cruel and suspicious Hieron, who had turned his court into the pre-eminent literary centre of its time – Pindar, Simonides, and Aeschylus were all long-term guests – Dionysius I, as Vincent Cronin tells us, was a man of lowly birth and no great moral standards, who was addicted to literature and to drama above all. It is said that he wrote tragedies and poems incessantly, though acclaim remained elusive. Why this was so we cannot verify, because all his writings are lost. A certain Philoxenus was imprisoned in the stone quarries for refusing to applaud the tyrant's poems. At the completion of his sentence, he was invited back to the court and asked to give his opinion on his ruler's latest creation. According to legend, he beckoned to a member of the royal

guard and exclaimed: 'Back to the Latomia with me, then!'
Dionysius I appreciated his ready wit and Philoxenus was
pardoned.

At the Athenian festivals, Dionysius I mostly came away
empty-handed. Occasionally he won the third prize, rarely,
the second. But the summit of the winner's podium was
denied to him. 'For the mightiest ruler of Greece, for a
tyrant whose power was no less than that of the great King
of Persia,' writes Cronin, 'this was a galling humiliation.'
And then, when the tyrant was already bowed by age, his
tragedy *The Ransom of Hector*, performed at one of the
smaller Athenian festivals, took the first prize.

Dionysius reeled with happiness, decreed a public
holiday and lavished food and wine on the entire population of Syracuse. The tyrant revelled until dawn at the head
of a monumental banquet. He had fulfilled his lifelong
ambition to shine, not only in life, but also on the stage. He
ate and drank so without restraint that in the early hours of
the morning a stroke carried him off.

5.

At the barber's on Via Roma. Colourless tufts of thin hair
fall to the floor around me. Salvatore Sparatore clicks his
scissors in a friendly manner. When I walked in, I said to
him: '*Barba e capelli, per favore, ma non troppo corto!*' But is
he keeping to that now?

A visit to the hairdresser's is a quick, simple, and proven way
of gaining access to a foreign city. I've been doing it since

forever. My best result was in Havana, where the barber was chatty, explaining the 'Fidel system' to me within fifteen minutes, and at the end of the procedure used a green pomade that left a pinkish shimmer on my parting. Sparatore is not so chatty. But customers still look in, fix an appointment or flop into a chair, and hold forth on the refuse collection, the incompetence of the new mayor, or the volume of last night's concert on the square in front of Castello Maniace.

In the past, musicians played in the *saloni* of Italian hairdressers to cheer up the customers, an age-old tradition. These small ensembles, most often guitar, tambour, and piccolo, sometimes mandolin and harmonica as well, moved from salon to salon. At some point, this custom died out and the barbers instead took to having small, pocket-sized calendars printed for their most loyal customers, which they would distribute at the end of each year. '*Omaggio Alla Gentile Clientele*' stood on the inner title page and then the months followed, each accompanied by a picture, mostly risqué, such as young ladies in hotpants on a Vespa, a biblical scene (Susanna bathing), or even the splendid décolletage of Gina Lollobrigida.

But Salvatore Sparatore needs none of this. His shop is in itself the attraction. The purest Sicilian Art Deco, unchanged since 1928. Heavy, yellow-painted peaches – or are they quinces? – carved of wood, on long, dull, light-green branches, hang on the already half-blinded mirrors set on opposite walls, with their infinity of copies.

'*La barba,*' Salvatore exclaims encouragingly and his cry does indeed herald the best part of the treatment. Lovingly my three-day-old stubble is lathered with spirited dabs of the shaving brush. The blade, restored to immaculate sharpness on a leather strap, glints, then scrapes over my skin, stretched in certain places by Salvatore's index finger and thumb. Then a lukewarm flannel wipes away the remnants of foam, before a final dab of delicious Proraso balm, which smells so intensely of eucalyptus and menthol that I feel transported into a state of blissful refreshment. Dazed but happy, I catch sight of myself in the mirror and wish Signor Sparatore *'una buona giornata!'*

6.

What do we need to feel happy? I ask myself this as I say my goodbyes to my barber. Only small things, apparently. But is that real happiness or just a small, delicious floating sensation, a brief exhilaration, an enlivening scent? For me, a 'real' feeling of happiness must also include the story of a long search, of exact looking, of something finally found and gained. This story of the search fades away over the years, and as it fades, the happiness pales as well. Wasn't my feeling of happiness in the first few weeks after I bought my apartment, as I stepped out onto the terrace each morning and gazed at the Ionian Sea, stronger then than it is today, almost precipitous, almost mighty? And hasn't it now become inward and almost flat? It's crazy, but even after more than seven years, I am still stopped each time I catch sight of the sea. It moves something in me, deep inside, and it dilates my senses, my breathing. Isn't this movement, I ask myself, the feeling of happiness I mean?

I can watch the sea, its colours, its moving surface, for hours, day after day. In the autumn the surface is often dove grey. Ortigia is the quail island, so its sea is quail grey. Later, it is nothing but a fat blue band, heralding the cold, dark half-light that the moon spills onto the swell. Only in summer is the sea blue or green: dark blue, deep blue, brutish blue, craggy blue or near to shore, a Caribbean green, arsenic green, like glass, like woodruff jelly. A wind smooths a path across the roughened water. The green loses its shimmer, grows dull, the 'breast of a slain peacock', as George Seferis described it in his lovely poem 'The King of Asini'. Often, in the evening, before the sun has vanished behind the Hyblaean Mountains, a breeze springs up, barely perceptible, a breath of air that at first ruffles the water, which loses its light, turns pearl grey, ash grey, quail grey, and then begins to search for indigo. Rarely, only after days of heavy rain, the streams of the Ciane and Anapo, swollen into torrents of water, push their silt into the great harbour with such force that a vast brown-green cloth spreads itself out in front of Plemmirio and only after days of mingling with the salty blue does the sea find its colour again.

7.

Do people who live surrounded by water ask themselves with greater emphasis or greater curiosity who they are? And who or what they belong to? I don't believe it. If they did, every islander, every captain, sailor, and fisher would be a metaphysician. I know island-dwellers who are more inclined to flee, who are happy to leave their island with its restrictions behind them, just as many a 'mainlander' cherishes the recurring fantasy of seeking refuge and seclusion on an island.

Plainly, there is something in island existence that draws us in, but can frighten us too. Is it because the beautiful and the terrifying, as several poets maintain, come from the same source, the sea? Besides, Ortigia is a special case, being an island that is connected by two bridges to another much larger island. It is, if you like, island-ness squared!

Writers seem to have a special sensorium for the allure of islands. It begins with Thomas More, who could only imagine his *Utopia* on an island. Countless authors followed, from Daniel Defoe to Adolfo Bioy Casares. And the literary figures who have visited Sicily are legion: from D. H. Lawrence to Ezra Pound, from Johann Gottfried Seume to Eugen Gottlob Winkler and Peter O. Chotjewitz, from Guy de Maupassant to André Gide, from Rabindranath Tagore to Sigmund Freud. Raymond Roussel slipped away in his room at the Grand Hotel et des Palmes in Palermo. Almost exactly a hundred years earlier, August von Platen died in Syracuse in the arms of a servant of Baron Landolina. As I sit in the little café by Fonte Aretusa, tracking the unceasing motion of the ships across the great harbour, I think of this unfortunate poet from Ansbach, who is better known here than in his native Germany. One of the large streets that runs past the Archaeological Museum is named after him. Via Augusto von Platen. He never had to leave the island.

8.

Baron Lucio Tasca di Lignari has a palace in the city, a large wine estate, a yacht, a significant collection of autograph manuscripts, and three hunting dogs. But he loves a simple place to eat and drink. I am sitting with him in Pizzeria Bianco Pepe on Piazza del Precursore.

'I know why you think this wall is the most beautiful in the world,' he says. We have been talking about the exterior wall of the cathedral, with its four Doric columns bulging out into Piazza Minerva. The capitals of eight further columns from the Temple of Athena are visible some way up. 'In front of this wall,' says the Baron, 'and otherwise perhaps only in the interior of the cathedral itself, you have the clearest sense of the history of Syracuse. For 1,600 years, it was one of the leading cities in Sicily and, for part of that time, one of the leading cities in the world.' He shoves a piece of pizza diavolo into his mouth. 'Few cities in the ancient world were so admired as Syracuse for their location, their buildings, their works of art. Few cities experienced so many strokes of good and bad fortune fused together, few cities could boast such a star cast' – here his voice quavers in a lower register – 'Theocritus, Gelon, Archimedes, later George Maniakes, later still Caravaggio ...' It would not take much for him to mention the name of his own dynasty here, but with a gulp of wine, he brings himself back under control. 'When I walk into the cathedral and see the columns of Athena, a sense of great continuity thrills through me. Do you understand that? Even the Arab conquest of the city in 878, which ended the era of ancient Syracuse and began her decline into provincialism, makes no difference to how I feel. This thrill inside me.'

'But how do you handle so much past?' I ask him. 'Doesn't it weigh on you, such a heavy burden?'

The Baron ventures an aphorism. 'The truly great cities are distinguished by the taint of their decline. It's a kind of retrospective condition of their greatness.'

I am silent for a moment, then try another tack: 'I mean the Sicilians, the people here in Syracuse. How do they handle it?'

'A great deal has been written on this subject. Our island's history and its position between the Ionian and African seas fuel insecurity. This insecurity underlies our entire existence and makes us capricious. The religiosity, all these processions, a certain fatalism, apathy and violence – all these, I'm afraid, are characteristic.' He nods sorrowfully.

The high branches of the bougainvillea that grows up the rough façade of the San Giovanni Battista church sway in the evening breeze. Monteleone's dog yaps. We order another Grillo.

'I'm sure you've read plenty of Leonardo Sciascia,' says the Baron. 'This Sciascia, he loved a line from Pirandello. He often quoted it: "You must know, that the likes of us are walking around with something like three watch chains in our heads. The serious one, the civilised, and the mad."'

'All mixed up together?'

'No. But the serious chain permits us to look back at our demented history and still be proud.'

'But you have stifled the greatness of this history your-selves. There are the columns, the temple in the cathedral, a few old foundations, there are remains of this and that, but these things on their own can't generate real meaning, nothing sensual.'

As I am speaking, I suddenly regret that I, a 'foreigner', am speaking to the Baron like this. He parries me immediately: 'Many of us have memories that are very much alive. There are moments when remembering the past becomes the present.'

And then the Baron goes a step further: 'For us, yes, sensuality and decline are intimately bound together. But we avoid living under the spell of what is past. There is a passion here for the life of today, no matter how forlorn it may be.'

9.

I had to think about what Tasca di Lignari had said for a long time. Not just what he had said about the nature of his fellow Sicilians, but also his observations about the cathedral. This monumental Greek temple, modified and rebuilt over and over by the Byzantines, the Arabs, the Hohenstaufens, the Normans, and the Baroque-addicted Italians, and the square which it dominates, the Piazza Duomo, form the natural centre of the city. Unlike Sicily's other Greek cities – Selinunte, Agrigento, and Segesta, all of which are fields of ruins today – in Syracuse the new has been built onto the old in a sequence of layers that are visible to this day, most obviously in the cathedral, the Athenaion. Some of these layers have been uncovered, to the benefit of the whole building. So, for example, it is only recently, a few decades ago, that another Doric column was freed from where the Byzantines had walled it in. This broken column, once the corner column of the entrance area of the temple, is now tucked inside a long, narrow sheath of stone: it is as if your eye steps into a tall, narrow space, in which the column stands as it has always stood.

The Baron had a similar formulation: the history of the city is symbolised in its cathedral. This monument has seen it all: erected in 480 BC by the tyrant Gelon to celebrate victory over the Carthaginians; shamelessly looted by the Roman governor Verres; consecrated as a Christian church in the Byzantine period; deconsecrated and converted into a mosque under the Arabs; rebuilt by the Normans; then finally swathed in baroque finery in the eighteenth century.

The cathedral lies at the very heart of the city. It is still a place of devotion, but less and less. Mostly it is a pulsating social centre that never rests. Every day natives and tourists mingle and parade on the steps of the church. The residents of the new town in particular come here when their work is done and bring the Corso to life, loving and admiring the sights of *their* city. Perhaps they are all amateur historians, like Giuseppe Monteleone, like Gaetano Tranchino, like my barber.

10.

When the British writer Lawrence Durrell visited Syracuse's cathedral in 1975, he fell into raptures: 'Start with a Greek temple,' he notes in his travel book, *Sicilian Carousel*, 'embed the whole in a Christian edifice to which you later add a Norman façade which gets knocked down by the great earthquake of 1693. Undaunted by this, you get busy once more and, completely changing direction, replace the old façade with a devilish graceful Baroque composition dated around 1728–54. And the whole thing, battered as it is, still smiles and breathes and manifests its virtue for all the world as if it had been thought out by a Leonardo or a Michelangelo.'

Some 175 years earlier, this superb building, which enthrals me afresh every time, failed to bewitch that celebrated walker Johann Gottfried Seume. Quite the opposite. In his travelogue of 1802 he notes: 'Minerva has had to make room in her temple for St Lucy. They have dealt with the building in the customary fashion and from a very fine temple, they have made a pretty poor church.' But Seume may not have been so wrong about that. The heavy, frankly cumbersome baroque elements in the nave were not removed until the 1920s, at the behest of the antiquities authorities, and it was only then, with its space purified, that the Doric temple regained its dignity, its rigour, its pre-eminence.

Whenever the German literati talk of Syracuse, Johann Gottfried Seume is always the first writer they think of. He inspired some authors to write their own stories, such as Friedrich Christian Delius, who, in his book *The Walk from Rostock to Syracuse*, has a waiter in East Germany set off to Sicily in Seume's footsteps. Seume's *Walk to Syracuse* went into a second edition immediately after first publication and grew to be a best- and long-seller. True, the book is pretty clunkily written, in a series of letters largely devoid of stylistic subtleties. But what fascinated readers back then was the sheer physical feat of hiking several thousand kilometres and, even more, that Seume, unlike Goethe and other self-improving travellers of his time, was not in search of some ideal of the antique world, nor its sensuality, nor even the 'free' life, but instead ruthlessly enumerated the evils of society, lashed out at the corruption of the clergy, and in general cast an unforgiving eye on everything he experienced. Upon arriving in Syracuse, he saw – as, later, did the historian Ferdinand Gregorovius – the vast field of ruins of the former megalopolis and spent a great deal of time in the *latomie*, the 'terrifying prisons of the Athenians'. The quarry by the Capuchin monastery, very close to Grand Hotel Villa Politi, was for him 'the largest, most terrible and most hideous' of any prison anywhere.

11.

Seume was only one of many writers to visit Syracuse. Let's start with Pindar, who came to Ortigia around 470 BC and composed several odes here, among them the 'Sixth Olympian Ode for Hagesias of Syracuse, Winner of the Mule Race'. Scholars of Ancient Greek believe it is in this poem that Pindar was best able to capture the spirit of Syracuse.

> Tell them to remember Syracuse and Ortygia,
> where Hieron rules with untainted sceptre and straight
>   counsels,
> honouring crimson-footed Demeter
> and keeping the festival of her daughter of the white
>   horses,
> and the feast of mighty Zeus on Aetna.

Four centuries later, Cicero came. Although the great age of the Greeks had long since passed, he praised the city in the highest terms. In his speeches *Against Verres*, the Roman governor of Sicily who had carried off countless works of art to Rome by extortion and direct violence, Cicero excoriated this art thief and, by winning the criminal trial against him in around 70 BC, greatly enhanced his public reputation. In his section on Syracuse, Cicero not only accurately describes 'the greatest and most beautiful of all Greek cities', but also itemises every work of art Verres had plundered. Thanks to the skill of Cicero's descriptions we can construct a precise picture of how the Temple of Minerva (the Roman name for Athena) was decorated. In the cella, for example, there was 'a glorious painting' of the cavalry battle of Agathocles against the Carthaginians. Verres had it removed and took other murals as well. Cicero addresses the court with eloquent rage: '[Verres] transferred the adornments of the virgin Minerva to the house of a prostitute. He took away besides this from the same temple twenty-seven of the most beautifully painted panels, on which were images of Sicily's kings and tyrants'. He comes to the doors of the Temple last: 'On the double doors were motifs meticulously executed in ivory; he took care that all were stripped off. A most beautiful face of a Gorgon, encircled by snakes, he ripped out and carried away.' Cicero's speeches repay the reading not just for his description of the plunder and portrait of the monstrous Verres, but also because he sketches out an exact picture of the structure and extent of the city and its five districts, named as they are to this day: Tyche, Achradina, Epipolai, Neapolis, and Ortigia.

Syracuse had many English-speaking visitors. Samuel Taylor Coleridge came from Malta in 1804, hoping to free himself in Syracuse from his opium addiction – which went spectacularly awry. In 1847, Edward Lear swung by on his Grand Tour. Ezra Pound alighted with his fellow poet William Butler Yeats at the Hotel Roma, opposite my barber on Via Roma. Pound's wife was disparaging about Ortigia; she sent home a postcard of the Fonte Aretusa and called the island 'a trifle of the East'.

The German and Austrian authors were scarcely less notable. Otto Weininger came to Syracuse in the summer of 1903 in the midst of a profound depression, after the publication of his book *Sex and Character* in Vienna had not been met with the impassioned interest he had expected. On 3 August, he wrote to Vienna: 'Syracuse is the most peculiar place in the world. I can only be born or die here – not live.' He did not elaborate on what he meant by these obscure lines. In another letter on 19 August, he recounts a trip up the Anapo by rowing boat, 'to the source, the famous Ciane' and enclosed flowers from a papyrus sedge. He was fascinated by the long, rigid, green stems which splayed out at the tip into a wheel of delicate gossamer, like the explosion of a small green firework. Like Seume, he climbed Etna. 'The imposing shamelessness' of the mountain alarmed him. 'A crater reminds me of a mandrill's backside,' he recorded in his notebook. In the same year, at the age of twenty-three, Weininger took his own life at Beethoven's death house in Vienna.

Sigmund Freud, who had declined to advocate for Weininger's manuscript, travelled to Sicily in 1910 and put up at the Hôtel des Étrangers with his travelling companion Sándor Ferenczi. We should also mention, among many other visitors, Ernst Jünger, who stopped off in Syracuse in 1977, as you may read in his diary, *Seventy Gone*. Like Pound and Yeats before him, he visited the Archaeological Museum and lingered in front of the Venus Landolina. He found it quite plausible that Guy de Maupassant had fallen in love with the statue: 'There is a relationship between archaeology and *décadence*, Art Nouveau in particular.' Jünger did not elaborate on this rather vague claim. The repressed eroticist was captivated by something else in the sculpture: 'the way in which the folds of the drapery merge into the ridges of a shell.'

12.

Some days on Piazza del Precursore I feel like I am on the set of a film by Pasolini: the smells of the café on the corner, the peals of church bells, the wail of a Vespa, a muddle of voices, the put-putting of motorbikes, and in amongst it all, what gifted supporting actors! Monteleone, the carefree pianist, plays his electric keyboard so heartrendingly loudly that tears spring from the eyes of elderly ladies on the street. Clara, the depressive shop assistant, having risen from her bed, appears on her balcony with her two whip-thin cats, who have nothing but contemptuous glances for Ronny, Monteleone's dog. Beneath them, at street level, the small man with Down's syndrome carries out his patrols while grey and ginger cats loll on the battered rooves of cars.

Monteleone hobbles out onto his little balcony. *Finita la musica?* I wave to him. He waves back. He once told me how he had bought this apartment, in which he still lives, way back in 1974, when he was a young police officer recently transferred from Catania to Syracuse. After his wife died and his son moved to Milan, he stayed on alone in the apartment and set up a veritable music studio in one of the deserted rooms. Giudecca was a pretty run-down area back then, but he had grown fond of it. 'In 1974,' he says, 'Piazza del Precursore was completely empty. A bit run down, but beautiful all the same. There were two cars: mine and a friend's Fiat 500. No restaurant, no tourists.'

His conclusion: '*Il tempo cambia tutto.* Time changes everything.'

'Do you want some more music?' he calls up to me across the square. 'Yes!' I say. 'The music of the future. Please.'

13.

I have been here so long now that I am able to look at some things as if I had written them myself. When I am sitting in Caffè Minerva and look out at the façade of Hotel Roma, I say to myself, this pink is my pink, these shutters are my shutters, which I open to look down at myself.

Little by little Caffè Minerva has become my favourite café. It is run by a lovely couple, a Sicilian man from Palazzolo Acreide and an amiable Australian woman with a penchant for old ceramics, glassware, vases, ornaments, and earthenware baking dishes. She decorates the shop windows not with almond biscuits and *cannoli*, but with Art Nouveau-style carafes and old glazed bowls. As you approach the café, which stands on the corner of Piazza Minerva and Via Roma, you think at first it's an antique shop. It's not until you've gone inside that you see the finely curved, generous counter of dark-red wood, the huge, glittering espresso machine, and the glass étagères bearing every kind of *dolci*.

Two paintings have fascinated me since my first visit, because they were out of the ordinary and gave the café a further distinctive note. Though they differ widely in size and hang in different spaces, you can recognise, nonetheless, in their relationships of colour and form and their impasto brushwork, that the same artist must have painted both. The smaller picture hangs directly behind the till. It shows a person sitting on a rounded rock, daydreaming as they read a book. The larger, far more exciting picture hangs in the rear section of the café and is surely meant to depict the Minerva itself. The curved counter and the drinks bar are clearly recognisable. Two figures, entirely held in a surreally deep green, sit boozing at a round table. One looks like a feminine Bacchus, naked, with breasts and a substantial belly, but with a face of classically 'Greek' regularity. The other is in half-profile, in a city suit. Our gaze is led outside, under an imagined blue vault. The Doric columns, which bulge out of the wall of the cathedral, complete the picture on the left-hand side. A yellow afternoon light pushes its way through from the cathedral square and bathes the town hall – or is it the Baron's palace? – in a sulphurous yellow glow. The perspective is extraordinary; the colours, with their lush triad of virulent yellow, algal green, and the deepest of blues, are more extraordinary still. The first time I saw this picture, I felt as if I'd been lowered into a grotto made of surreal elements, in which, nonetheless, character-istic features of Syracuse are clearly visible.

The Australian, Signora Ricutto, who alternates sitting at the till with her husband, the Sicilian I already mentioned, and her two daughters, is the one in her family who is interested in art and beauty. She answers my questions eagerly. Yes, both paintings originate from the same painter, Gaetano Tranchino, who has just turned seventy-nine. If I would like, she would happily take me with her to his studio on Via Nizza, not far from here. She loves his pictures. They depict their own distinct world, governed by their own distinct sense of time. She would like to buy another picture from Tranchino, perhaps even two, and – she repeats the offer – will happily take me with her.

The style of the two pictures is so unmistakeable that I ask her if the enormous picture in the foyer of the Grand Hotel Ortigia is not also the work of this Tranchino. This image, perhaps three by five metres in size, depicts in weather-beaten candy colours Syracuse's great harbour, the Porta Marina, and Lungomare Alfeo with its long avenue of trimmed carob trees. A steamer is setting out from the dock. A huge smoke plume made of black stone gushes from its funnel.

'Yes,' says Signora Ricutto, almost happily. 'Isn't it a wonderful picture? For me, it encapsulates the whole of Ortigia.'

I can only agree. Many years ago, when I booked a room in this hotel and for the first time saw this picture installed behind the reception, it enchanted me at a stroke. It has an oneiric quality. It shows a Mediterranean world, which does not and yet could exist.

We decide to visit the painter on Via Nizza the following day.

14.

To anticipate straightaway: our visit to the studio of Gaetano Tranchino ended with the purchase of a painting.

The studio is located on the ground floor of a stately baroque house, where Gaetano and his wife also live. He gave us a very friendly welcome and heaved one picture after another onto one of the easels that stood around the elongated space. Little by little the world of the painter emerged, made of unreal elements that we nonetheless think we know: a stormy and then again calm sea, the waterside promenades, Paseo and Lungomare, archaeological fragments, fractured honey-yellow columns, huge steamers, pedestrians, dogs, slender women vanishing and reappearing between plump palm trees. It is a topography that has since become familiar to me, but in colours and shapes I have never yet seen and which seem to obey other laws of movement and stasis.

I told Tranchino that I recognised Ortigia in his pictures and that he had given the old myths of Syracuse new life.

What did I mean by that, he asked.

This is not a frozen world, I replied, and that is a miracle. It is a warm world, a heartfelt world, a world which hides secrets. I asked him whether he felt close to Giorgio de Chirico and his brother Alberto Savinio and he answered yes. He revered Alberto especially, he said. But his most powerful partner was his memory. Reminiscences of childhood – his parents' house and garden, the air that moved a pale blue curtain, walks on Lungomare, the dolphins in the sky – had given birth to a complex dreamworld.

Signora Ricutto fell in love with a picture of a young man roaming through a garden. He is smoking; he looks like a dandy; he holds a book in his hand.

'That's a *viaggiatore*,' said Gaetano. 'Travellers are always showing up in my pictures. Even if they're the kind of *viaggiatore* who never really leaves the island, they're still journeying through life.'

'And the villa in the background?'

'That's a memory of the building where I spent a lot of weekends as a child. It's in Plemmirio, not far from Hotel Minareto. An enchanted house, though it's overgrown now. From the first-floor balcony you could see out across the entrance to the Porto Grande to the silhouette of Ortigia.'

In the picture the house looks like a toy villa. There are toy ships and toy cars in Tranchino's pictures as well and the sea has toy waves.

The picture I purchased is a pure dream picture. It shows the sea of Syracuse in the evening. A vintage, green-painted car is turning the corner on Lungomare. A ship approaches on phosphorescent waves. But no ship ever entered a harbour like this and its proportions are much too big for this harbour. Fundamentally, nothing in this picture makes sense. Reality is elsewhere. Probably the reason I cannot tire of looking at it.

15.

In Syracuse there is no avoiding Arethusa. This nymph decorates the silver ten-drachma coins which were in circulation 2,400 years ago, in the time of the tyrant Dionysius I. Poets sing of her. We find her on wine labels and postcards. Stockbrokers' and cafés adorn themselves with her name. The 500-lira bank note, first printed by Italy's central bank in 1966, shows her classically beautiful head in a pin-sharp engraving, with earring, hair grip, and necklace, while all along the lower edge of this *biglietto di stato*, four dolphins amuse themselves with merry leaps.

One of the first to extoll Arethusa was Ovid in his *Metamorphoses* – unsurprisingly, because her story is also one of transformation. Her tutelary goddess, Diana, known to the Greeks as Artemis, had at first protected her from the lecherous assault of the river god Alpheus by throwing a large cloud around her, concealing her from his sight. But when Alpheus persisted, Diana transformed her protégée into water and sent her under the sea to Syracuse:

Diana cleft the earth. I, sinking down,
Borne through blind caverns reached Ortygia,
That bears my goddess' name, the isle I love,
That first restored me to the air above.

The savage pursuit, just before the nymph's transformation into a spring, must have been what most fascinated Ovid. It is as if he put himself in Arethusa's place as he wrote. The most beautifully Ovidian line is: 'His gasping mouth was blowing on the ribbons in my hair.' Today, as I sit in the little café opposite the spring, I hear the heavy breath of the river god. I hear the gasping of the white horses of Lipica, I hear the gasping of my father as he talks about the war, I hear the gasping of Ingrid Thulin in Ingmar Bergman's film *The Silence*, I hear all the gasping and silence of the world.

16.

'This coin,' said the Baron, 'is one of the most beautiful coins in the world. It enchanted Ezra Pound and his friend William Butler Yeats alongside him. The pair of them had brought large magnifying glasses with them from London to inspect Syracuse's numismatic collection.'

We had been talking about early depictions of Arethusa. Here too Tasca di Lignari demonstrated his expertise. It was important for him that this head of Arethusa with the dolphins swimming around it was in fact the head of Persephone, also known as Kore. The head and neck jewellery and how well they are depicted are, he says, decisive in any valuation. Not long ago, at an auction in Munich, one specimen fetched 50,000 euros.

'Three times the estimate!' exclaimed the Baron excitedly. This was down to two things. One, that her earrings and head jewellery were exceptionally fresh, without the tiniest crack or faintest signs of wear. Two, that this coin bore the signature of its die-cutter: 'EYINE'. The famed coin-maker Euainetos had manufactured it and evidently was so proud of the result that he furnished the drachmas with his signature as they were going into production.

No surprise to me that Tasca di Lignari at this point quickly added that he owned a 'small, modest' collection of coins, which he would be pleased to show me. Though it was not here in his city palace, he said. He kept it safe in the country, on his wine estate, which we should visit at some point anyway. He had set up a spacious *studiolo* there in a tower, containing a part of his collections: autograph manuscripts relating to the history of Sicily and astronomical instruments, as well as the aforementioned coins.

These faded remnants of Sicily's aristocracy fascinate me. Naturally it was Don Fabrizio, the massive, melancholic prince in Giuseppe Tomasi di Lampedusa's *The Leopard* who lit the fuse of my interest. Syracuse had been as much a playground of the nobility as Palermo. Philipp Joseph Rehfues, who journeyed to Sicily in 1804 in the company of Karl Friedrich Schinkel, vividly depicts Syracuse's aristocratic social world. Rehfues pays particular tribute to Tommaso Gargallo, the *marchese* of Castellentini, and the Baron Don Mario Landolina, who cared for the dying Count August von Platen and was acclaimed by von Platen as the 'most learned man in Syracuse'. But the house of Tasca di Lignari doesn't get a mention. Which only made me more curious about the history of this noble family.

'Isn't it odd that I'm so in love with Sicily?' I said to the Baron. 'There are so many things about it to criticise, today as in the past. The exploitation of tenant farmers in the century before last, the injustices perpetrated by the aristocracy, perhaps even by your family, the inhuman working conditions of the miners in the sulphur pits, the role of the Mafia, the rubbish on every exit road ...'

Lucio Tasca di Lignari interrupted me: 'There are always things that are revolting' – yes, he said *revolting*! – 'and there are always people who fall short of the image we associate with Sicily. But this image, this idea, survives nonetheless.

And other people come forward who will embody this idea again.'

'But what exactly is this 'idea' you are talking about?'

'It's not about the light, the landscape, the heroic coastline, the sumptuous architecture. It's about something else, some kind of historical continuity, stretching over several thousands of years. It's unheard of, unique, and yet not inexplicable. It's a passing on of forms, beauties, convictions. Fundamentally, in spite of all the ruptures, it's a vast recycling, that has carried on working to this day. You can read this continuity in the walls of the cathedral, but you can also taste it in the pasta that has been prepared here since time immemorial, or even see it in some of the faces you come across on Via Roma.'

It made me think of Monteleone. He embodies this continuity. And Syracuse too is a place of continuity, a place that takes note of decline, of death, and where men and women stand in unbroken relation to those who lived before.

17.

The sea was in a rage tonight, pelting the whole city with rattling spray. I could hear the din all the way up in my room. The elements found no peace until morning. It felt to me as if the breath of the waves had finally recovered its great regularity.

'Aren't we all just fragments?' Monteleone called merrily up to me from his balcony. 'And some of us fit seamlessly together,' he continued in his distinctive voice.

'You mean, you and I fit together?' I called down to him jokily.

A soft wind billowed his tatty dressing gown, magenta with a frayed collar. I knew exactly how he had arrived at his theme. Two days ago the local newspapers and radio had been reporting on the 'rediscovered *kouros*'. Syracuse's Archaeological Museum houses the torso of a youth from the Greek Archaic period, found in Lentini and made of marble from Paros – which means, the finest. This statue is one of the jewels of the museum. The only misfortune is that this *kouros* long ago lost its head. For almost as long, people have speculated whether a head in the museum in Catania, the *Testa Biscari* – named after the Prince of Biscari, an archaeologist, who discovered the head in Lentini in the eighteenth century and bequeathed it to his home city of Catania – might not be the missing head of the youth. And now, just recently, the body and the head had been assembled into one *kouros* for the first time. The head, with its triple wreath of hair, battered nose, and mysterious smile around its lips, now stands on the slender, armless trunk. If the photos in the newspapers are to be trusted, their artfully lit staging leaves no doubt that what has finally been reunited belongs together, having been separated a mere two millennia. The *kouros* seems life-sized, calm, almost stiff and yet enlivened by some hidden movement, originating in the rightness of its proportions.

'Shouldn't we visit this handsome young man in Catania? A group outing, Giuseppe?'

Monteleone gestured to his legs and the crutch propped against the balcony railing. 'Unfortunately, I'm not so good on my feet anymore. But this handsome man is supposed to make the journey to Syracuse this winter. We'll have a look at him here!'

'Good. Then we'll check whether his neck operation has been a success.'

'And whether his smile is still his smile.'

Monteleone's words make me think of the terracotta *korai* in the Paolo Orsi Archaeological Museum here. Every one of them exhibits this cryptic smile, ironic and voluptuous, and yet at the same time content with itself. In my diary I had named it 'the smile of Syracuse'.

18.

'And what do you do, exactly?' Gaetano asked me, when I visited him once again in his dusty, cluttered studio on Via Nizza.

'I write poems,' I said. 'Right now, I'm trying to write poems about Syracuse.'

'How lucky you are, to be able to build word-dwellings!'

'That's nicely put. Houses made of words. But aren't you doing the same? Building a world out of shapes and colours?'

'Oh, I'm afraid I've exhausted my universe. It's too private. I want to say more about Sicily, not just my dreams, my longings' – he paused artfully – 'and my disappointments.'

I said nothing.

'Do you think that Sicilians have a characteristic mood?' he continued and then straightaway answered his own question: 'There is something serious about them. You could almost say: un-cheerful. Even the few outbreaks of cheerfulness are tinged with darkness.'

'But in your paintings, darkness is a rarity. Perhaps the jet-black steamer on the glass-green waves? Or the smoke that looks as if it were made of dark stone?'

'My friend, the photographer Ferdinando Scianna, has always said I can't paint smoke. I'd be better to leave it alone. He says that when some huge boulder of granite squeezes itself out of the funnel, my paintings look like Magritte's.'

'Monsieur Magritte,' I murmur. 'Your paintings have the seriousness of dreams. The seriousness of the Sicilians is alien to them.'

And I added, to myself, 'Thank God!' *Grazie a Dio.*

19.

Ortigia is a stone city. Susceptible to sunlight. In the morning it's white, in the afternoon yellow, in the evening cinnamon. Because it is made of stone, with no earth, no grass, there are hardly any insects and the few there are, are snapped up by lizards on the walls, or in the air by arrow-fast swifts. I have counted the palms of Ortigia. Four neat date palms stand on the small square in front of Palazzo Bellomo, casting sharply pointed, feathery shadows on a flaking, pale-pink wall. Two lofty palms with a profusion of sagging, withered fronds protrude from the open gothic nave of San Giovanni Battista right next to my apartment. The priest has the palms cut back but only after long intervals of two or three years. On the site of Apollo's Temple, very close to the market, there is a cluster of five or six palms. In the courtyard of the Papyrus Museum a slender fan palm, perhaps twenty-five metres tall, sways next to a sturdy date palm. Four colossally tall king palms hem in Piazza Pancali on both sides. And eight palms have recently been planted at the Porto Piccolo, on the way to the bar of the restaurant Area M. I have counted thirty palms.

The most painful loss for me is a pair of magnificent date palms that stood in the garden of the archbishop's palace on the cathedral square. You can admire them in old photos. They made their way up into the sky from a thicket of oleander bushes and gave the whole square a shimmering, oriental panache. It is said that red palm weevils, pests that multiply themselves with uncanny speed, hollowed the palms out from within and killed them off. For a long time I hoped that the archbishop, undoubtedly an affluent man, would replace the palms. Apparently, a single, fully grown twenty-year-old palm would now cost over 4,000 euros, but for the still wealthy church in Sicily, that's a trifle, a bagatelle. I have occasionally thought that someone should launch a petition, a mini-referendum, but no one seems to want to do anything about the loss of the palms. Signor Sparatore shrugs his shoulders, his scissors clacking.

20.

I want to go back to the catacombs of San Giovanni. This church from the sixth century, the earliest in all of Syracuse, was erected over the crypt and subterranean necropolis. I visited the catacombs soon after I first arrived in Syracuse, but later my impressions were rather overlaid by the catacombs of Palermo, which are incomparably more dramatic.

There you wander among hundreds, even thousands, of embalmed corpses arranged by age, sex, and rank and are astounded that so much decaying biological matter can yet retain so much 'poise', so much of a 'human expression'. Back then in Palermo, as I strolled among the mummies, I was oddly reminded of the Teatro dei Pupi, the famous

Sicilian puppet theatre. Aren't these corpses, with their frozen, thoroughly unnatural gestures, the marionettes of the kingdom of the dead? Perhaps, rather than the episodes from *Orlando Furioso*, of Roland in his rage, they are acting out Ovid's *Metamorphoses*? From dust to yet more dust.

The catacombs of San Giovanni in Syracuse, as I am now confirming, are something entirely different. There are no mummies, no corpses. They've all been cleared away. Broad, underground streets meet at junctions quarried out of rock. The grand scale of the complex may be explained, says our guide, by the fact that from 313 AD onwards, Christian burials no longer had to be held in secret. Over the years that followed, the catacombs evolved into a 'normal' burial ground under the earth, with individual graves and family tombs, which increasingly were furnished with ornamentation and inscriptions. Almost all the inscriptions were chiselled into the stone in Greek. As a whole, this empty and extensively ramified complex attests to the grandeur and prosperity of the early Christian community in Syracuse.

I want to ask the guide, a young, wiry character who speaks good English, some more questions on mortuary practices, the inscriptions, and the layout of the burial chambers but she does everything hastily, as if she is out of time and the next tourists are already expecting her. I try to give her a tip, but she brusquely refuses.

21.

Today the cat killed a tiny lizard on the terrace. Presumably it broke its neck, before biting into its belly. Some of its entrails have leaked from its side, in front of its right hindleg. Its spine has sprung out as well, up to the point where it becomes the tail. The markings on its scaly skin are very beautiful, a matt green with a band of irregularly patterned black and white down its sides. The delicate head is entirely unscathed, with small, lidless, black-bead eyes.

Do lizard parents grieve for their dead child? I contemplated the slender carcass for a long time and then threw it in the toilet.

22.

It is already late in the year. The thirteenth of December, early evening. An unusually large number of people are standing around on Piazza Pancali. I let myself drift onto the bridge as part of the crowd. The atmosphere is festive. Expectation hangs in the air. The procession in honour of St Lucia, patron saint of the city, should be arriving any moment. A young man next to me says that they set out from the basilica in the new town three hours ago. They're at the lower end of Corso Umberto and will shortly be crossing the bridge towards their final destination, the cathedral. The procession seems heavily delayed. Forty men carry the gleaming Lucia, drenched in silver on her golden tabernacle, fixed to a huge wooden frame, called the *vara*. You have to apply to be a bearer, and be of good standing in the community. It is said that in the past young men also had to swear an oath that they would lead their lives in the spirit of St Lucia from then on.

At around 9 p.m., the procession arrives at the bridge leading to Ortigia. Immediately there are loud firecrackers, flaring lights in the sky, a spray of stars: a magnificent firework display has begun, launched in her honour. Many of the people in the long body of the procession, men and women, young and old, are carrying huge, very thick candles. At first, in the twilight, I mistake them for stakes or the trunks of saplings. The candles are almost as large as the people carrying them. The candle-bearers are walking barefoot; some of the less courageous have put socks on. The pavement must already be cold by this time in the evening. But the fireworks are so beautiful that they ease the mortifications of the faithful. *Giochi di fuochi.* The fireworks for St Lucia are great sheaves of light that hang in the black sky for a long time, then slowly, very slowly, tilt towards earth and burn out. Over and over, fiery circles and garlands of light prevent the extinguishing of the world. Thunderous and yet also airy, glittering creations, for a moment, they blind you.

On and on we go, in groups, great clusters of humanity. It gets tighter and tighter, until near to Piazza Duomo it is barely possible to move forward. The crowd has formed an impenetrable wall. I feel this: that everyone is waiting for a miracle. Finally, around eleven, as Lucia reaches the portal of the cathedral, she is turned once on her axis – an inspired directorial touch! – so that now, with her silver dagger deep in her throat, she looks out over the vast crowd below her as she disappears backwards into the Temple of Athena.

The crowd, still breathless, now lets the black night in. It breaks into groups and grouplets, trickles away down the streets around the cathedral – Roma, Cavour, Minerva, Logoteta – a little exhausted from all the glittering commotion and at the same time calmed by the knowledge that the saint is entirely alone in the great stillness of the cathedral.

I pass Caffè Minerva on my way home. It's still open. I treat myself to a *caffè*, an *amaretto*, and a *baci*. Its motto, wrapped between the chocolate and the silver foil, reads: 'The freshest lips give the warmest kiss.' From Seneca, allegedly.

23.

Santa Lucia continues to occupy my thoughts in the days that follow. I discover in a book on the early history of the city that she was executed on 13 December 304 AD, during the persecution of the Christians under the Roman Emperor Diocletian. An early martyr, who swiftly became very famous. In the countless depictions of her that exist, she either has a dagger in her neck or carries her eyeballs on a small platter. Thus the two most widely disseminated versions of how she died: stabbed and then beheaded, or blinded and then beheaded.

For a long time her body was preserved in Syracuse, in the basilica that bears her name. In an octagonal prayer room, below ground level, you can still see the hollow in the rock that was the saint's first resting place. In 1039 a Byzantine general named Maniakes carried her remains to Constantinople. From there the Venetians took her to *la Serenissima* and buried her in the church of San Geremia, where she rests to this day. She was 'loaned out' to Syracuse on a single occasion, for a week in December 2004 – that is, 1,700 years since her execution. According to the local newspapers, all of Syracuse was seized by joyful rapture.

The procession in honour of their saint is to Syracusans more important than Christmas. *Natale* means red Advent stars and red underwear and deep red floodlighting at the headquarters of the jeweller Massimo Izzo on Piazza Archimede. But true rapture, fireworks, glittering devotion, and deep ecstasy – all these only St Lucia can conjure.

24.

From time to time I need a change of island. Ortigia becomes too small for me and I cross over to the 'mainland'. From Syracuse train station to the Station Bar is a journey of 230 paces, about 100 metres. When you walk it, you are moving through time: from 1871, when the station had its topping-out ceremony, to the 1980s, when the catering and left-luggage office were moved out of the station and the Station Bar was created to take over those roles. The interior of the bar is not exactly cosy. A few square metal tables, woven plastic chairs, scuffed black-and-white floor tiles. The current tenants seem to have no time for decoration and to know nothing of the hunger for interpersonal warmth, let alone epicurean warmth. I've never been able to find out whether this establishment was called the 'Station Bar' from the beginning or had this name slapped on it at a later date in a reckless wave of Americanism. At night, above the grubby, never-folded-away parasols, a green area of the façade, about the size of a ping-pong table, boasts in white neon letters: 'STATION BAR' and then beneath: '*PASTICCERIA, ROSTICCERIA, GASTRONOMIA, PANINERIA*', as if the owners could not be satisfied with just one or even two descriptions for their business. And to the left is another board, in blue, on which yellow letters announce to weary travellers '*DEPOSITO BAGAGLI*' and below that, in impeccable English translation: 'BAGGAGE ROOM'.

If I should ever find myself directing a film, I would, without a shadow of a doubt, have the opening scene play out in this provincial train station – and the final murder would have to be committed in the Station Bar. The train station, with its two graceful storeys, has a honey-yellow façade with arched windows framed in white. A canopy arches over platform *uno* on slender cast-iron columns. Once a day, very late in the afternoon, the *treno notte* stops under this shelter, an elegant black train that is reputed to run from Agrigento via Syracuse, Catania, and Messina, then climb up the entire boot as far as – unbelievable! – Milan. The journey, we are told, lasts twenty-two hours.

When I first caught a train here, a standard regional service to Catania, I noticed a plaque of pale marble installed between two of the three entrance portals. The donors of the plaque name themselves first of all: the state railway company and the municipality of Syracuse. Reading further, we learn that it was installed in honour of 'Sebastiano Vittorini, 1883–1972, man of letters and railwayman, who was stationmaster of this building.' And then come two rather cryptic concluding lines: '*Dove lo scrittore Elio incontro Rosa Quasimodo*' – 'where the writer Elio met Rosa Quasimodo'. An author who can be identified in a public place by just his first name must be very well known, and Syracuse produced no more famous writer in the twentieth century: Elio Vittorini, the stationmaster's son, author of the classic *Conversations in Sicily*, editor, commentator, and a tireless figure on the Italian left. And Rosa Quasimodo, also the child of a railwayman, was the sister of the poet Salvatore Quasimodo, who in 1959 became the second Sicilian after Luigi Pirandello to be awarded the Nobel Prize for Literature. So this plaque harbours a veritable love story, which only the initiated can entirely understand. Andreas Rossmann found the following passage while researching Rosa Quasimodo's memoirs, published in 1984: 'One evening in August he was waiting for me as arranged at the window of his room and I ran barefoot the entire length of the station roof and climbed up to him in the apartment.' The two were married in 1927; their marriage lasted twelve years.

My favourite time to be in the Station Bar is Christmas. As I look across at the station from one of the smeary windows, I think of Elio and Rosa. Near the year's end there's more business than usual and our simple-minded host has even tacked a few red caps to the wall. The clientele consists of one or two bus drivers on a break, rail passengers waiting for the next train to Augusta or Lentini, some careworn staff from the nearby offices, and a few prostitutes, who nip over in glittery flip-flops from the little hotel on Viale Ermocrate and treat themselves to a drink between tricks. These women have, as my old barber would say, long since left the 'full bloom of womanhood' behind them. The petals around their eyes and mouth are thoroughly crinkled. And now an African woman blows in at the same time. 'Where to? Where from?' I hum to myself. 'From Mali,' she tells me. She speaks excellent French. She raps her thick rings against her glass and says: '*C'est l'amour qui frappe.*'

Then, into the silence: 'Adeline'. That's her name.

25.

Another regular stop on the 'mainland' is the fish restaurant Onda Blu. A third is the bookshop Zaratan, set up by the publishing house Ventidue and named for a magnificent, antediluvian sea turtle. In its premises on Corso Umberto I, Zaratan at first sold only its own products: postcards, note-books, and, most of all, books describing features of the area, designed with exceptional care and a strong feeling for beauty. But the publisher soon grew tired of the day-to-day running of the business and wanted to concentrate entirely on his publishing. By happy chance, his sister, a photogra-pher named Maria Vittoria Trovato, had just then returned from Berlin and wanted to take over the shop. Along with her friend, a violinist with a passion for new music, she broadened the range and in short time made Zaratan the most exciting bookseller in the city. Now, alongside the more commonplace stock, you could find abstruse volumes of poetry, playful children's books, opinionated treatises on aubergines and citrus fruit, and thoroughly strange books from Italy's smallest publishing houses, as well as vinyl records hand-pressed by obscure artisans in Turin.

It was there, not long ago, that I discovered a slim volume entitled *Tentazione di Siracusa*. The author is Jacques Derrida. From its foreword I gather that in 2001 he was made an honorary citizen of Syracuse. This booklet consists essentially of the speech he gave when he accepted this honour.

Why 'temptation'? It makes me think of medieval paint-ings. *The Temptation of Saint Anthony*. But this is not about sex, about carnal attraction. The title surely alludes to the power, grandeur, pomp, and unrivalled beauty of the city in its heyday. Many must have been tempted to set sail for Syracuse and try their luck in the Manhattan of the ancient world, a metropolis of half a million people. One who succumbed to this temptation was Plato. The renowned philosopher, bored in Athens and making little progress with plans for his Academy, travelled three times to Syracuse over more than two decades. In his speech, Derrida refers to the philosopher's repeated journeys and his search for a foundation for the ideal political system he wanted to make into a reality.

His first journey was in 388 BC. The encounter between the political thinker, by then already very well-known, and Dionysius I, the most powerful ruler in the western Mediterranean, did not go well, because the tyrant was a long way from Plato's ideal of the 'philosopher king'. In his *Life of Dion*, Plutarch tells us that, although the volatile Dionysius learned to tolerate Plato's conversation 'as a wild beast [does] the touch of a man', the situation darkened by degrees. According to Plutarch, Plato began to expound his ideas of virtue, courage, and justice at a banquet given in his honour. When he considered humanity as a whole, Plato said, it was the tyrants who possessed these qualities the least. Dionysius I heard in these pronouncements a rebuke aimed in his direction and at the same time had the feeling that everyone taking part in the feast agreed with Plato. Eventually he lost his composure, Plutarch writes, and asked Plato why he'd come to Sicily at all, to which Plato answered that he was searching for a virtuous man. Dionysius I replied: 'Well, you don't seem to have found one!'

Feeling that his life was now in danger, Plato embarked on a trireme the next day. Stories that Dionysius I asked the captain to murder Plato or sell him into slavery at Aegina probably belong, however, to the realms of fantasy.

Dion, an important adviser to Dionysius II, the son of the old tyrant, got to know Plato during his first, abortive visit. Dion was an enthusiastic proponent of Plato's teachings and wanted to bring him and his new master together to devise a constitution for the Greek cities in Sicily. So, in 367 BC, Plato came a second time to Syracuse, twenty years after he first made the journey. Was he blinded? Utterly blinded? And if so, by what? He must have perceived this Greek metropolis in the western Mediterranean, even more strongly than before, as the antithesis and alter ego of Athens, a place where it now seemed possible to take the first steps towards the ideal political system that he had described in his recently completed book, *The Republic*. But this journey too ended in fiasco. The chemistry between Plato and Dionysius II simply did not work. The philosopher's euphoria quickly gave way to deep scepticism. Dion was sent into exile. The tyrant's court favourites began to plot against Plato, until his situation grew so precarious that he travelled back to Athens. And so it is utterly inexplicable that six years later, in 361 BC, Plato showed up back in Syracuse. What siren call was he hearing this time? In the very last conversation that Dionysius II had with Plato, the tyrant is supposed to have said: 'You will be saying many bad things about me to your colleagues in Athens'. To which Plato is supposed to have replied: 'Heavens, no!

It is unthinkable that we should have so little to discuss in the Academy that we would find the time to mention your name.'

26.

An addendum. At the beginning of 1934, the famed classical scholar Wolfgang Schadewaldt, a wonderful translator of Sappho and Homer, is sitting on a tram in Freiburg. Martin Heidegger, who has recently become rector of the university there and just had his first skirmishes with the authorities in Berlin, gets on. 'So, Martin,' Schadewaldt greets him, 'back from Syracuse?'

27.

And yet, does anything remain of this city, the mightiest political entity the Greeks ever managed to establish, a city of great pomp, but also of endless sieges and ruinous campaigns, does anything remain beyond these witnesses in stone? Is there a myth glimmering still? An idea? Or has that early glory dissolved into dust and ash? Do schools and universities talk of Syracuse at all? Do the young say to themselves: Why Greece still? What's the use of believing in the ancient world? What meanings for our present can you gain from that anymore?

Recently, a friend who was visiting me on Ortigia said: 'There's so much past here that there's hardly any room for the future. I feel like I'm sitting in a glamorous Grand Hotel with plaster crumbling off the walls.'

'I'm afraid the plaster went long ago,' I replied. 'But the Syracusans don't look back wistfully. They live among ruins and they are understandably worried about the future. They just keep struggling onwards. Struggling from one decline to the next.'

My friend said nothing.

'I'm exaggerating a little,' I said, 'as is my wont. And I have to admit I don't exactly know what makes young Sicilians tick. Probably they know that their traditions, the traditional sectors of the economy included, are all played out, that the fatalism of their parents achieves nothing, and that they have to keep up with digitisation and sell their hearts – and their past – to tourism.'

28.

I also often discuss with my friend Gaetano Tranchino whether the past can shed its lifeless museum-ness and be incarnated in present-day people and pictures and events. That's how we came to the subject of Marpessa and whether she is the Arethusa of today.

We had been talking about Gaetano's friend Ferdinando Scianna. Gaetano said that Ferdinando was not just a damned good photographer, he was a damned good writer as well. He often composed brief texts to go with his pictures, vivid portraits in words. I had already heard of the photographer Scianna back before I had an apartment in Ortigia and before I knew Gaetano. The C/O gallery in Berlin had mounted an exhibition of the work of Magnum photographers. This was the first time he caught my attention, with passport-photo-sized photos of a young woman with exceptionally intense eyes. There was a row of three large prints made from these contact images, which were marked up with strokes of red pencil. Below them, on a white placard, stood: 'Marpessa, Bagheria, 1987'. Bagheria is a suburb of Palermo, well-known primarily for the Villa Palagonia with its baroque monsters and grotesques. Well-known also because every traveller of the eighteenth and nineteenth centuries stopped off there. And ultimately well-known, though this I didn't learn until later, because Ferdinando Scianna had published a cult book – nowadays hard to find – *Quelli di Bagheria*, in which he had made portraits of all the inhabitants of his birth city.

Marpessa fascinated me when I first saw her at the C/O, but I didn't think very deeply about her. For me she was a woman from Bagheria, a young Sicilian woman with a dark complexion, an almost Greek profile, strong eyebrows and an equally strong lower lip. To me she seemed, from that first time I set eyes on her, the prototype of Mediterranean womanhood. Later, when I wanted to purchase a print of this photo through the Magnum agency, I discovered that Marpessa had been born in Amsterdam to a Dutch mother and a father from Suriname, that she had the bourgeois name Marpessa Hennink, and that in the 1980s she had been a world-famous model, tied by an exclusive contract to Dolce & Gabbana. Even when I learned all this, my dreams did not fall to earth. Had I experienced something similar to Leonardo Sciascia, who wrote that, for him, Marpessa had been transformed 'in a Pirandellian way' into a character? Even Scianna said that he did not perceive her as a model. For him, she had been a young woman – he used the word *ragazza* – who was 'unfathomably beautiful'. Through her, he said, he had told a story about 'the relationship between womanhood and Sicily, a true fiction, a fictional truth'. Her name – *Marpessa* – is the title of a book he published and which has the subtitle *Récit*, a story. I have been unable to find it in any second-hand bookshop in the world. When I told Gaetano this, he just rolled his eyes and whispered: 'Marpessa'.

29.

The Red Moon restaurant has been something of a 'hidden gem', perhaps because, although I heard about it early on, I still, years later, haven't actually found my way to this rough-and-ready seafood joint at Riva Porto Lachio on the Porto Piccolo. Now the time has come. I am meeting up with the translator Dora Suma and her husband Alberto on a Saturday, the day when every Syracusan heads out and splurges.

Straightaway we find ourselves in a film by Federico Fellini. The petty bourgeois, hipsters, ill-matched lovers, and ladies of doubtful provenance in their middle youth are sitting at wobbly tables in some kind of car park next to a tented area. The behaviour of one group of three *ragazze*, directly in my sightline, is especially conspicuous. Two of the three 'ladies' are on the plump side, with a solidly built quality that matches their thickly applied make-up. One has crammed her bosom, the precise extent of which you would not want to know, into a red chiffon blouse, which is itself stuffed into a baggy black skirt. The second has squeezed herself into a casing of dark lizard skin, all imitation, with purple spaghetti straps. The third is showing an enormous quantity of skin. Two thick, fleshy bulges protrude from her other-worldly neckline, held in with difficulty by two bowls of black fabric, against which their owner repeatedly rubs the display of her mobile phone to clear it of greasy prints. Her back, shoulders, and arms are covered in greenish tattoos. Her stiletto heels are at least fifteen centimetres high. Her ordinary presence has an unfaked quality that outstrips our 'authenticity'. She takes non-stop selfies with her two comrades. Bursts of laughter. The three eat for all they're worth and drink wine to the limits of their bladders. A thoroughly cheerful, cheering spectacle. Dora, however, who was educated by the Ursuline Sisters in Ortigia, finds it all rather too much. And Alberto, a Calabrese, acts horrified, though I can't entirely make him out. The waiters do the bare minimum, slam bottles onto the table and bring giant, purple octopuses, their round heads like red light-bulbs resting majestically on a tangle of thick, sucker-covered cables.

The view from our restaurant table across to Ortigia is blocked by delivery vans and pick-up trucks. We really are dining in the middle of a car park. In the past, a small ferry regularly travelled back and forth between Riva Porto Lachio and the marina on Ortigia. Now, at this hour, we see fishing boats a long way out, trying to lure fish with powerful lamps. Giuseppe Monteleone has told me that the men who go fishing at night have made it their habit to sleep with their wives in the late afternoon. Then straight from bed to cutter and out into the darkening sea.

30.

After the debauchery of the Red Moon, today the sky and sun today seem plain, almost austere, Ionic. I walk to Arethusa's spring and can just see the nymph taking a bath in the overgrown pool. The expanse of sea remains empty.

There are days when the island seems grey and hunched. But today it shines. Today I find it hard to believe that this island could feel anything like self-pity: that its great days are over. That its theatre is no longer so large, its bus terminal is broken and Corso Gelone, once the new town's grand boulevard, is blighted. And that the sea is unfurrowed by the cruise ships upon which the *sindaco*, the mayor, had set the entirety of his hopes.

The best are the overexposed days of August. The people look as stiff as lizards in the sun, except that they sit at the iron tables of cafés and from time to time guide a *negroni sbagliato* to their lips. They look like people who have lost their faith in shade.

The loveliest, deepest shade of all is on Via Logoteta on late summer afternoons. Setting out from my apartment on Piazza del Precursore, I like to walk the length of it, coming out onto Via Roma refreshed, then in a few steps I am past my barber's and at Caffè Minerva. But I don't just like Via Logoteta for its deep shade in midsummer. In every season it fits the image of a Sicilian alleyway in a bad airport novel. Clothes lines criss-cross over your head and hanging plants spring forth from between iron balcony railings, only made more lush, it seems, by the lack of water. There is the Courtyard of the Greeks, *Ronco li Greci*, and a few workshops, where artisans work wood on noisy machines and wipe sawdust from their brows. There are no feral dogs and rarely a watchful, half-starved cat, and yet a great many dishes of cat food next to pots and pot plants and tin buckets in half-open doorways, behind which televisions jabber and blare.

31.

It's not just cheerful Adeline. It's not just the sellers from Gambia and Senegal who want to market their leather goods, dirt-cheap jewellery, and poorly carved elephants with a tenacious flood of words. There simply are more and more immigrants. They stand out in the streetscape. The number of African refugees has risen. At the entrance to the immigration authorities' office, not far from the Talete car park on Ortigia, they stand around in groups, waiting for papers, stamps, signatures, fearful of an adverse ruling. In their faces I can read their uncertainty over what happens next. To be without papers means to be without prospects. If they are lucky, they are allowed to stay and become the slaves of the twenty-first century. Many of them toil in the tomato fields of Pachino.

In the past, they were allowed to remain for thirty days until the office had decided for or against their asylum application. In unclear cases a *foglio di via*, a deferral for fifteen days, would be granted to allow further investigations. But that was years ago. The rules have been changed a dozen times since and no one really understands them anymore. Everything has certainly become stricter, the exceptions are more sharply worded, and yet Sicilians on the whole have shown a striking generosity. When Matteo Salvini, the far-right leader of the Lega Nord and for a short time Italy's interior minister, forbade boats carrying refugees from landing in Italian ports, many Syracusans spontaneously fixed banners painted with '*Porti aperti!*' to their balconies. Open harbours!

No one knows how many illegal immigrants today are battling their way through life in Syracuse. Some are mobile hawkers; some find a home in restaurant kitchens; some clean the homes of the rich. There used to be Africans who polished the windscreens of drivers waiting at traffic lights and hoped for tips, so Giuseppe Monteleone tells me, but not anymore.

Giuseppe and Dora Suma also say with a certain verve that until the early 1990s, Ortigia was a hotbed of prostitution. *Tempi passati*. No longer do red lights glow at the entrances to the little houses on Lungomare di Levante, which has since been restored and poshed up. Italian men call the Black prostitutes *lucciole*, fireflies, which sounds almost tender. Banished from Ortigia, they relocated to the train station. The nearest turf, I'm told, was Corso Umberto I, but it was too busy. Many are deported and return again and again. Today many ply their trade outside the city. You see them on the edge of fields, at intersections, on folding chairs in front of abandoned *cabanas*. It has become a discreet business. Many fireflies wear dark-green T-shirts and brown-green skirts, which makes them even less visible, lets them disappear into nature.

32.

Today I took a book with me to Caffè Minerva, an anthology of texts about the Mediterranean. I found these lines by Roland Barthes: 'The hairdresser, the shoe-shine boy and the bath attendant are three frequent products of the Mediterranean countries; as dirt cannot well be eliminated, it is adorned, it is covered in a glaze; to this end, no effort is spared: they are more miserly of water than of coatings: pomades, waxes and cosmetics abound, taking the place of soap, as oil did for the Ancient Greeks.' Barthes noted this more than eighty years ago in Athens at the height of summer. Maybe there was a lot of rubbish lying around. Whereas Ortigia is tidy. Still, I'm going to read this passage out to Salvatore Sparatore, my barber. Because he is an artist of the pomade. He has never betrayed his age to me. Eighty? An intensely yellow sign surfaces sporadically in his shop window, '*Vendesi*', as if he had had enough of the scissors and foam and ill-tempered customers and wants to retire. This sign spooks me. When I ask him about it, he mumbles: '*Non significa nulla.*' It doesn't mean anything. Right before my eyes he takes the sign down and tucks it away between tattered copies of *L'Espresso*. And then a few days later the sign reappears.

Recently, as he was giving me a shave, he told me he had visited relatives in Naples and on the return journey taken the *treno notte*, the night train, from Naples to Syracuse. Immediately I had a vision of those glossy black bolides, which had made such an impression on me when I saw them halted at the *stazione* in Syracuse, and which had straightaway awakened a desire to travel all the way from Rome to Syracuse – or in the opposite direction.

'How was it?' I asked him, with foam at my mouth.

I had already many times imagined such a train journey. A dapper, uniformed conductor fluffs up my pillow, stretches the smooth sheet still smoother, asks me if I would like a *prosecco* or a *vino bianco*, a *verdicchio*, before my *cena*. He brings over the newspaper; he is professionalism and affability personified. Sometimes on my imagined train, a female conductor, a sort of stewardess, drops by as well, shakes her bottle-blonde hair and brings me towels and a bottle of water.

'How was it?' I asked him impatiently.

Signor Sparatore sharpened his razorblade and said he had enjoyed the journey very much. What it would have been for me, a nostalgic or literary experience, it had not been for him. He had a hatred, I learned, of budget airlines and so much preferred an anachronistic mode of transport like the railway. Besides, for him the time passed in a flash. There had been two other stops before Messina, at Salerno and Reggio Calabria, but he had not woken up until the train was no longer pounding and lurching, its wheels were still, and it found itself, both carriages and engine, on the ferry.

'How long does the crossing to Messina take?'

'Oh, barely quarter of an hour. But as we arrived into the terminal at Messina, I had the feeling: I am back in my world now.'

33.

Looking out from Ortigia on very clear winter days, you see a broad dome of snow spread out above the houses of the new town. The effect is unreal. You rub your eyes.

Ah yes, it is the snow-covered summit of Etna. When the writer Terézia Mora climbed Etna, also in the winter, she emailed me a photo, which showed nothing except an enormous official information board and a few snow-covered bushes behind it. On the board, on the dark-brown background that is the signature colour for tourist attractions throughout Italy, stood the words, '*Comune di Sant'Alfio*', then beneath that, '*Monti Sartorius*' and then beneath that, 's.l.m. 1667m'. Plainly it refers to some secondary craters that bear my name and stand at 1,667 metres above sea level. I was flattered but didn't really know what to do with it.

Much later I discovered in an edition of *La Lettura*, the excellent weekly literary supplement of *Corriere della Sera*, an advert from a publishing house in Catania promoting a voluminous book with the German title *Der Aetna*. Beneath the title, though difficult to make out in the blurred photograph of the book cover, were the words: 'Collected Manuscripts of Wolfgang Sartorius von Waltershausen: With a Selection of His Drawings.' Now I was wide awake. On the internet I quickly discovered that this Sartorius lived in the nineteenth century, taught geology in Göttingen, and had been one of the most eminent vulcanologists in the Europe of his day. He spent more than a decade conducting fieldwork on the slopes of Etna, mapped every lava flow from the volcano, including those from centuries past, as far as they could be measured and records existed, and left behind thousands of drawings and sketches. He was a maniac, a geology nut, who spent more time in Sicily and Iceland than Göttingen. Now that 'Sartorius' meant more to me than just my own name, I questioned the jeep drivers and mountain guides who took tourists to the summit of Etna about him and all of them knew his name and all of them knew that Sartorius had done a great service with his studies into the volcano's moods. Even the old men in the café in Sant'Alfio knew what he was about. 'But Etna is good-natured,' a farmer at the counter said to me soothingly after one of the numerous eruptions had once again covered the street in front of the café with a finger-thick layer of dust and ash. 'It's just letting off pressure and then overflows a bit.' The man next to him, who turned out to be a retired teacher from the area, concurred. 'Etna is a gigantic living being,' he said. 'It lives, it shivers, it rumbles, but it doesn't do anything to us.' On my journey back to the station in Catania to catch the train to Syracuse, the driver spiritedly explained to me that the volcano was not only a destroyer. It was also the great *madre*, he said, which gives life. That's true, and every book on the subject says the same: the volcanic rock breaks down into dark soil over decades and becomes exceptionally fertile. A stroll through the markets in Catania or Syracuse will convince even the most blinkered sceptic. Nowhere else grow such magnificent lemons, reddish-tinged blood oranges, fragrant mandarins, and green-violet pistachios as here on the slopes of the mighty mountain.

34.

Etna is not so omnipresent in Syracuse as it is in Catania. This may simply be because at a distance of fifty kilometres the giant is only rarely visible. On one occasion, when I was visiting the *Due Colonne*, it loomed over the plain, like a black, almost perfectly triangular silhouette against the reddish evening sky. From the terrace of this restaurant, you can see the delta formed by the Anapo and Ciane rivers, the two stumps of Doric columns for which the eatery is named, and – in extremely clear weather – along the coast as far as Catania and Mount Etna. Another time, in winter, on the bastion opposite Hotel Gutkowski, I doubted my eyes as I gradually became aware of the white, faintly glittering summit over the rooves of the new town. The air that day must have been exceptionally transparent.

This image has remained on my inner retina, unerasable. Even years later, a paragon of flawless brightness. A luminous sea, very pale house fronts, an almost white, unstreaked sky and in the middle of it, this unreal white peak. A shimmer. A cold glow. A wedding crinoline. The Canadian artist Jeff Wall was the first to mount photographs on lightboxes and so produce a tremendous brilliancy. For me, the wintry, white summit of the volcano above the rooves of Neapolis has become a lightbox picture like his.

35.

Sicilians love to compare cities. A friend of mine from Palermo, on a visit to Syracuse, says to me: 'You have to admit that our city, however much of it lives on only as a memory, is more exciting, as well as more aristocratic than Catania or even Rome.' And then he adds, as if to wound me: 'To say nothing of Syracuse.'

I tell him that I see no great differences between the Sicilian cities. Boundless excitement reigns everywhere. The local newspapers outdo each other with tacky or even frankly grim stories. Three out of every four politicians are corrupt, they say. Funeral processions interfere with the running of local businesses everywhere and whenever the Post Office's heap of undelivered mail grows too imposing, i.e. hill-like, it simply dumps it in the sea.

My friend is about to protest but I don't let him get a word in. I say: 'All of which is especially true of Palermo. And yet in spite of all that, I love Palermo very much. I would want to live there, if there were no Syracuse.'

36.

Many years ago, when I lived in New York (a distant descendant of Syracuse), I was fascinated by a recurring feature of *The New Yorker* magazine, which appeared always at the front of the issue, straight after the culture guide. It was – and still is – called 'The Talk of the Town'. Here big-name scribblers, the finest pens of the East Coast, lovingly applied themselves, as if with a magnifying glass, to the details of city life. No matter the theme – corruption, building projects, criminal trials, drugs, tearjerkers, vice – it was wrapped in their fondness for the city. Perhaps with this book, I am aiming at something similar, trying to assemble a portrait of Syracuse from these fragments of perception, as if under a magnifying glass.

In Syracuse today you would search in vain for a city magazine of any kind. There is a regional daily newspaper, *La Sicilia*, which publishes across the whole of Sicily, and has regional sections, including a 'book' of four to six pages for Catania and Syracuse. It is good that this poorly produced, sensationalist, and gossipy local news exists, because it pays attention to the details and in this way forms a kind of last defence against the total standardisation of how lives are lived. Time and again I find stories in it, which, trivial though they may appear, tell me that one of the greatest distinctions between Sicily and our northern latitudes is the different relationship to time. Here there is no rush. In its place is nonchalance mixed with curiosity. Like the local section of the newspaper, every shop in Ortigia is an exchange for news. Everyone trades stories for minutes at a time with the pharmacist, with the woman on the checkout at the supermarket, with the cheesemonger at the market. This elastic handling of time seems to affect even the media. Is this to do with being an island? A friend reminded me of Pirandello, who claimed that Sicilians have an excessively insular mentality, because the sea isolates them and makes them alone. That may be right, but it does not touch on this sense of time, which you encounter throughout southern Italy and as far north as Naples – namely, the sense that the passing of time is not such a weighty thing at all.

37.

Though he lives in an old townhouse on Via della Giudecca – right near me, in other words – I see Carlo Coniglio only rarely. I have got to know him at his studio – iwhiteplus – as an exceptionally elegant and well-educated young man. My estate agent introduced me to him because he considered him one of the city's most promising designers. After I bought my apartment, Coniglio designed a new kitchen for it. The old one was decayed; the edges of the drawers were peeling off and the interior of the dishwasher looked as if a fire had raged in it. Coniglio's design was cheerful; I liked its dazzling colours and quickly had it implemented.

Carlo Coniglio. What an excellent name! Charles Rabbit. Incidentally, a name that suits him well, because Carlo always looks like an extremely fashionably dressed, nervous rabbit. In the last year, by way of compensation, he has acquired a Great Dane. Not the giant edition: a size medium. Its fabulous coat is a fawn colour, a light grey-brown coat, the coat of a fox that has been tamed for too long.

When I bump into him now, he is Great Dane-less. 'Where's your dog?' I ask him.

'Ugh! Ortigia is stony!' – he stresses the word 'stony' with a fit of vehemence. 'This city is no good for dogs that need somewhere to run. I've loaned him to some friends in the country for a week.'

'Shall we have breakfast together?' I know he has breakfast every morning at around eleven o'clock in Hotel Roma on Via Roma and that every lunchtime he eats with his father in the new town, usually at the Onda Blu fish restaurant.

Carlo agrees.

We sit down in the breakfast room of the hotel. It was once the best on the square, where Ezra Pound and William Butler Yeats stayed to inspect the Temple of Athena in the cathedral and the famed coin collections of the *Museo Archeologico*. The hotel understands how to preserve its old elegance. A round table covered with a white cloth awaits us. The atmosphere is bright; everything is fragrant with efficiency; the waiters know what needs to be brought. The rabbit dismantles a *cornetto vuoto*, an unfilled croissant, destroying the beautiful, matte glaze on its back with a soft smacking of his lips, then plucking the slightly greasy pastry from inside and forming it into little beads.

'For the pigeons?'

'No. They're the souls of living beings that we don't know yet.'

'Oh dear. Are you ill?'

'What do you mean? I just like playing around like this.'

'What are you working on? Do you have any commissions?'

'I've had an enquiry about something big. But I'm not enjoying it. Unfortunately. It's a shame!'

I look at him expectantly.

'It's for this new building at the entrance to Castello Maniace. They're building a modernist structure there right now, all glass and mirror-polished steel. Its roof is a giant, retractable wave. Inside there's going to be a restaurant, a café, a bar that goes on forever, and I've been invited to join a pitch for the interior design. But this building, right next to the austere square fort of the Hohenstaufen, it's alien. It's egregiously misconceived. It's no fun wondering how to furnish a place that you reject in your deepest soul.'

He sets off again: 'With jobs like this, I like to be guided by the exterior architecture. But it's so full of cheap effects that it's pretty much paralysed me. "Designer's block!"' he exclaims in English. 'On the other hand, I wonder if I shouldn't design brutally austere tables and chairs, to refer to the clean lines of the castle, its superb concision, its intolerance for fripperies.'

I've not been to the tip of Ortigia for several weeks. 'So this new building is already there?'

'Yes, it's almost finished. It's bloated. Badly proportioned. I'm sure you'll find it just as execrable, just as out of place, as I do.'

38.

Castello Maniace was built between 1232 and 1240, in the reign of the Hohenstaufen Emperor Frederick II. With its strict, quadrangular plan and brawny round towers at its four corners, it recalls other of the Hohenstaufens' fortified buildings, the famous Castel del Monte most of all, of course, but also the Hohenstaufen castles in Catania and Augusta and the grandiosely forbidding, bunker-like hunting lodge in Favara, near Agrigento. Maniace stands right at the end of the long finger with which Ortigia points into the Ionian Sea. This southern tip of the island is an outstanding location geographically, offering perfect control over the entrance to Syracuse's great harbour. It is said that a temple to Hera stood here back in the time of the very first Greeks. Later, the tyrants erected their palaces on the same spot. The castle of today takes its name from the Byzantine general George Maniakes, who retook Syracuse from the Arabs in the pay of his masters in Constantinople. During the reign of Frederick II, the fortress served not just as a military garrison, but also as a royal palace. If contemporary accounts are to be believed, Frederick II visited Syracuse on at least three occasions.

One gains some hint of the imperial splendour in the castle's gigantic inner space, a hall held up by mighty cross-ribbed vaults resting on giant columns. The first time I walked into this hall, I was overwhelmed by its height, its magnificence, its proportions. Its very emptiness gave a huge spur to my imagination, which had anyway already been set in motion by accounts of the legendary peripatetic court that Frederick II, like a king of Oriental fable, maintained to accompany him. In his book on Italy, *Backlit*, Joachim Fest, normally such a cool writer, retells these accounts with gusto:

> At the head rode the Saracen guard, 300 men in gleaming armour, their saddlecloths studded with gems. A train of camels followed, lavishly harnessed and decked with silverware and bells. Led by solemn-paced eunuchs, they bore heavily veiled Arab slave girls on splendid chairs, the Emperor's 'Gomorrhan harem', as the Pope disapprovingly remarked. The four-horse teams with the treasure carriages, piled high with pieces in gold and silver, with sea silk and royal purple, were followed by troubadours and tumblers, jugglers and musicians. Only after them, at a measured distance, came the royal court itself: Frederick on horseback, adorned with the insignia of power and surrounded by senior dignitaries and by pageboys and servants in colourfully striped tunics. A red-covered float of scholars came next and a retinue of falconers with every kind of hunting bird, white and coloured peacocks, African ostriches, parrots and rare pigeons, then the hound masters with the straining pack and animal tamers leading lions and leopards, apes, bears and panthers on golden chains. The climax was the

elephant, which the Emperor had received as a gift from the Sultan, bearing a tower frame lined with shimmering cloth, upon which splendidly dressed Moors blew the signals on silver trumpets. In the rearguard came the packhorses, with the chancellery papers and the library.

Such a procession, in all its exoticism and majestic, fairy-tale character, must have profoundly excited the imagination of Frederick's contemporaries and indicated, almost by necessity, that Frederick was indeed, as Fest says, a 'Cosmocrator', a man with both the peoples and the creatures of the world equally at his disposal, entirely in line with his own dictum: 'Our reins run to the very ends of the earth.'

What a line! What a feeling of power! Here in Maniace, in this grand hall, which in the early Middle Ages must have brimmed with gorgeous ceremony and teeming bustle, here at the tip of Ortigia, with a view across to Plemmirio, which Virgil praised long ago in his *Aeneid*, I have a sudden sense of how much Sicily is the place where Europe began. In Syracuse and still more in Palermo, Frederick II tried to derive an entitlement to rule from the island's geographic situation and the antiquity of its culture: politically, as the midpoint of the world and culturally, as a meeting place between East and West.

This claim, but also this openness and readiness for co-operation and conviviality, never returned. The bastions that the Spanish powers erected around the castle in the sixteenth century are a vivid token of the loss. The Spaniards also lopped off the second storey above the grand hall, to offer a smaller target to the Ottomans' cannons. Now all signs pointed to hardship and war.

39.

I cannot see the castle from the terrace of my apartment, as it is hidden by various buildings and the dark, moss-covered nave of a church, but I can see the southern tip of Plemmirio, with the lighthouse that marks out the entrance to the Porto Grande. I mentioned Virgil. Here is the passage from the *Aeneid*:

> There is an island
> fronting the bay of Syracuse – over against Plemyrium's
> headland rocked by breakers – called Ortygia once
> by men in the old days. They tell how Alpheus,
> the Elean river, forcing his passage undersea
> by secret channels, now, Arethusa, mixes streams
> at your fountain's mouth with your Sicilian waters.

That nymph really is everywhere!

40.

The relationship between sea and ruins is strained, in Ortigia and every old city by the sea. We sense the conflict: the baleful unending reality of the sea and the fractured stone.

George Perros, friend of my poet friend, Lorrand Gaspar, said that the sea is the monument of all monuments. He also said: 'The sea is pure, undreamed-of irrationality.'

I cannot grasp this great expanse of water before my eyes and yet I do not want to fall silent.

Arrival

1.

Years ago, at an antiquarian bookshop on Suarezstraße in Berlin, I bought one of those old *Baedekers* in the hymn-book format, its cloth binding a deep wine red, not church black, but with an embossed gold title and marbled edges. The title is terse to the point of bold: *Mediterranean*. With the help of forty-three remarkably precise maps and forty-six stroll-inviting city plans, here is the entire Mediterranean travelled around, wandered around, sailed around. A glorious book. Quite possibly, my favourite book. The description of each city begins, before the naming of sights, with the section, 'Arrival by Sea'. On page 63, on the subject of Syracuse, we read: 'The steamers from Naples and Egypt drop anchor in the Porto Grande. The steamer for Tripoli berths by the customs office; that for Malta by the harbour train station.' The fact that the trains from Messina run to the station on the harbour is likewise noted, no matter that strictly speaking this has nothing to do with arrival by sea.

Barely ninety years later – the *Baedeker* in my possession was published in 1934 – and the 'steamers' are pretty much gone. A few plump ferries connect Catania with Genoa and Palermo with Naples and Salerno. But, as far as the movement of people is concerned, air has almost entirely replaced sea. It's a marvel that there is still the blackly gleaming *treno notte*, in which you may travel down the length of the boot, cross over to Messina, and then, having made it to Sicily, continue on to Syracuse and Agrigento, the end of the line. The largest of Sicily's airports is Catania. That's where I land, most of the time, so that I can get to Syracuse by bus or taxi in around fifty minutes.

2.

But first I must pass through the eye of a needle. This eye of a needle is named Caffè Parisi and it is one of the most wonderful *pasticcerie* in this part of the world. My stop there, before I travel on to Syracuse, is a kind of sweet initiation, a delicious ritual. This land of milk and honey is located on one of the main roads out of Catania Airport. The fame of the *dolci* fabricated here is so great, the aroma so much mightier than that of the kerosene, that everyone elbows their way in, everyone wants to feast: truckers and business travellers, sales reps and taxi drivers, passengers with long stopovers and mothers with their *bambini*, whining for *gelati*. The rest of us want a delicate, oven-warm puff pastry case stuffed with almond paste to go with the black, black *caffè*. Or the green glazed breasts of Sant'Agata, patron saint of Catania. These too are hotly craved. The crisp *cannoli con crema alla ricotta* that splinter under your teeth and the *cassata* enriched with orange-blossom water and crushed pistachios hurtle over the counter, as do generous slices of *ciambella al limone* and every variety of *croccante*, chopped almonds bound together by hard, caramelised sugar syrup. The knowledgeable writer Hanns-Josef Ortheil has devoted an entire

66

book to these Sicilian sweets, a voluptuous compendium, which I can only recommend.

I have got into the habit of fortifying myself at Caffè Parisi before my onward journey with a green breast or a *granita di caffè con panna* and buying more for my days in Ortigia. There are excellent pastry shops in Syracuse but Caffè Parisi is in a class of its own. And there's something else: this *Caffè* has spectacular wrapping paper. When I was young, there were times when I bought a record purely for its cover. At the Parisi, I buy more than I need, because I am a slave to their wrapping paper. Reddish aeroplanes in the style of a woodcut and old Sicilian carts dart about between multicoloured scoops of ice cream, *cornetti*, and *cassata*. A dusting of gold sharpens the colours. It trickles down onto every treat and makes them, wrapped in this paper, still more desirable.

3.

In Ortigia itself as well there is no arriving without a ritual. My first stop is the market on Via Emmanuele de Benedictis. It is the most magnificent, colourful, and richly fragranced place on the island. Here fruit and vegetables, courgette flowers and wild fennel, huge, yellow, pockmarked *cedri*, and deep-purple, almost black, aubergines are piled in heaps. White, green, and lilac-blue cabbages too. *Polpi* simmer in a huge pot, until the trader fishes them out one by one with a fork and deftly cuts them into manageable slices with a sharp knife. There are stalls for spices, nuts, and cheese, for *ricotta salata* and *ricotta fresca* and *ricotta al forno*. And twelve kinds of pecorino. The fish stalls are the most thrilling of all. There are four of them. The *Casa del Pesce* specialises in tuna and swordfish. You step into a large area under bright carbide lamps, looking past bloody 'swords' into at least a dozen colossal dead fish eyes. Nothing is more delicious, says my library of fish recipes, than a thin slice of swordfish, coated in oil, garnished with capers, parsley, and onion and swiftly grilled over charcoal.

I read in a dictionary that in Sicily there are multiple dialect words for swordfish: *spatu* or *pisci-spata* or, most beautifully, *puddicinéddu*, a word that the fishermen use of young fish, but which among Sicilians also generally means a small child who is playing the fool. Young swordfish can be very clownish. They turn somersaults or leap boisterously out of the water – just like a *puddicinéddu*.

Sicily's craziest market is the *Vucciria* in Palermo. The great Renato Guttuso has painted it. A gloriously teeming 'Where's Wally?'-style image. I'd love to own it and clear a wall for it in my *salotto*. The beasts of the sea romp about in the lower left section of the oil painting. A trader grasps a swordfish head. Silvery, scaly bodies curl in baskets. Shoppers weave along a narrow alley, on the other side of which are towers of fruit and vegetables – red peppers, fennel, lemons, bundles of fresh mint – and an entire blood-red side of beef dangling very insistently from a meat hook, next to preserving jars, wheels of cheese, a mighty mortadella, and then behind them more cascades of apples, apricots, nuts, onions, lemons again, the whole melee brightly illuminated by three carbide lamps. A ravishing, crazy picture.

Not long ago I found a rare catalogue of Renato

Guttuso's early work at Ortigia's market, which is itself a very successful replica of the *Vucciria*. In a novel move, an antiquarian bookseller has set up a stall right at the end of the market street, and now sells secondhand books on the history, cities, and art of Sicily every day, including issues of the magazine *Sicilia* from the 1950s and 1960s, which still exude a remarkable freshness and daring in their design. Here I also discovered a small-format book entitled *Vicolo sperduta*, about the alleyways of Ortigia, with black-and-white images by the photographer Carlo di Silvestro and a foreword by a writer I much admire, Vincenzo Consolo. In these pictures Ortigia looks scratched, crumbling, decayed. The pictures mostly show children in front of the dark walls of houses or bricked-up entranceways, playing joylessly in the lightless *vicoli* of the Giudecca quarter or in the *roncos*, the small cul-de-sacs, of Graziella. According to the copyright notice, the photos all date from 1995, but they seem older, as if they might also have been taken much earlier.

4.

'Ortigia was dark back then,' says Dora Suma. 'Morbid. Every façade whispered of decadence. Every wall of times gone by.' Back then means the mid-1980s, when Dora came back to Syracuse from Germany with her parents.

Her father had grown sick of Sicily and went first to Fiat in Turin and from there to Germany. He was a trained welder and worked briefly in a factory before he found a permanent position at the federal post office in Böblingen.

'My mother met him on the side of the football pitch in Böblingen,' says Dora. 'It must have been love at first sight.

That's the story they told me. And my mother got pregnant very quickly.'

'And that was you?'

'Yes. I grew up at my grandma's, who was a midwife. A wonderful, warm-hearted woman. My mother had to go to work. She didn't have so much time for me. But they were good years. I liked the little town. I was happy going to school. I loved my grandma. I didn't understand why my parents chose in 1984 to head back to Sicily. I was just under fourteen years old. We took the train from Stuttgart to Milan, then from Milan to Syracuse. On the line from Messina to Syracuse, I just cried.'

'When I first met you, Dora, not long after I arrived here, I took you for a German. Your aura is so blonde – and your German is flawless. I do wonder what drove your father. It was really such a huge decision, to take you out of school, tear the family away from everything you knew, from a secure way of life, and return to Syracuse. Just because he came from there and because his mother lived there?'

'It was hard for me. I knew Sicily from a few holidays but it wasn't my home. And there was no way it could be. I missed my girlfriends. Everything was different from in Germany. The food. The way people behaved. The light. The language. In Böblingen I had only spoken German. Suddenly there wasn't a word of it. But I didn't want to forget the language, even if now I had to exclusively speak Italian, at my other grandma's in Syracuse, in school, with all my relatives.'

'I have to ask you again: how do you explain their decision, to leave everything behind and try to re-establish themselves back in Sicily?'

'My parents thought that if I stayed, I would have become an out-and-out German. And that didn't fit with my father. And they also thought that the morals in Germany were too loose. I wouldn't have been protected enough. I would have been easy prey for German men.'

Here Dora chuckles.

'Which naturally was very funny, because I'd barely arrived in Syracuse when I met Alberto, we fell in love, and I was pregnant at seventeen.'

'But you were with the Ursulines in Ortigia, under their watch. How could that have happened? Were the nuns so lax?'

'I loved Sister Celeste. She taught me Italian. She understood the turmoil I was in, but that only made her try harder to drum some moral principles into me. On which point, you need to know that we were living in the new town. My journey to school every morning took me along Corso Umberto and over the bridge to Ortigia, past the Bourbon prison, which was still in operation back then, with a crowd of women clamouring at the iron bars, calling out the names of their imprisoned men. And the prostitutes still had their little establishments on Via Nizza. They sat in the doorway in their negligées, with their legs spread and the nuns would shout at us: "Don't look at the women! Look at the sea!"

'I was a special case at school,' continued Dora. 'In Syracuse, my mother mutated from a German into an American. Because I was blonde with green eyes I was called "the daughter of the American woman".'

There was something in that. Even before I knew her story, I could have imagined Dora as the head of personnel at one of the luxury hotels on Plemmirio or running the head office of some big company in the area. There is something very winning in how she conducts herself. In reality, she was working, when I first met her, as an assistant to a dentist on Corso Gelone. Later she set up her own business and now she works as an interpreter and teacher for struggling German students. Or she translates, as she did for me at the notary's office when I was buying my apartment. Little by little my friendship has grown with her and her husband Alberto, who works at the city's land registry. Because I have no car, they have taken me with them on trips to IKEA in Catania and, far more importantly, showed me beautiful beaches in the area around Syracuse, which I would never have discovered on my own. To this day I am grateful for how much they eased my entry into Sicilian life.

5.

Dora has a weakness for the actor Enrico Lo Verso. He actually is very good-looking: an Odysseus type, brown and sinewy with a flecked beard that curls into ringlets. A native of Syracuse, he has acted in countless films and shaken up several TV series. The women of Syracuse revere him. I once had him sign a book for Dora – short stories by Pirandello – and she was beside herself. In December 2016 he had awakened Syracuse's Teatro Communale from its long slumber with a monologue from Pirandello.

Friends who visit me invariably ask about the performances of Euripides in the Greek Theatre. They don't know that the city has two impressive theatres: not just the ancient theatre hewn from limestone and designed to take up to 15,000 spectators, but also the pretty municipal theatre, which stands at the corner of Via del Teatro and Via Roma and can hold just under 500 people, 200 of them in the plush red armchairs of the stalls.

'We have to bring this theatre back to life,' I tell my friends. 'It opened in 1872 with Gounod's *Faust* and was shut in 1958 with a performance of *Cavalleria Rusticana*. That's a long time ago and that's how long the theatre has been dead. There was an attempt to resuscitate it. With Enrico Lo Verso. It went pretty well. A short play was performed for five evenings. Then there was an evening of jazz, a couple of classical concerts, and it all ebbed away again. We have to take it in hand!' I exhort my friends, once again. 'Adriano, you take over the directorship. You speak Italian, which is vital. You can negotiate with the *assessore della cultura*. About grants. And you, Rüdiger – Ruggiero – you take on the advertising and the ticket sales. And I will crank up the café!'

'So how come the relaunch five years ago didn't work?'

'I don't know. The city has lost its educated bourgeoisie. There is no middle class any more. Nowadays everyone, or almost everyone, is geared to tourism. In summer people work endlessly hard, chasing after money. In winter, they're exhausted and have no interest in watching a play.'

Adriano raises a didactic finger. 'There is also another explanation for this deadlock, this hibernation. They say that the theatre is cursed. A Benedictine monastery stood where the theatre now stands, Monastero di nostra Signora dell'Annunziata, along with the palace of some Catholic worthy. All of which was torn down and the materials were used to build the theatre. There was some legal skirmishing, reputedly, at the end of which this Temple of the Muses stood on the site, in the neoclassical style that caused such a furore throughout Italy in the years before 1900.'

I am not giving up. 'There's supposed to be an openhouse day soon. You really need to see the theatre from the inside. It's a small, consumptive replica of the Palais Garnier in Paris. But it's pretty. And the stage curtain is genuinely magical. It shows Daphne in a wood populated with nymphs, a reference to the pastoral poetry that has its beginnings with the great Theocritus here in Syracuse.'

Finally my friends are catching the fire. I show them photos of the stalls and the painted domed ceiling.

'So, what might a season look like?' says Ruggiero.

'Chamber opera?' suggests Adriano. 'Looking at these photos, I reckon the orchestra pit is just about big enough. Schönberg's *Erwartung*. One-acters by Dallapiccola, Luciano Berio. That sort of thing.'

I tap my forehead with my index finger. '*Piano. Piano.* It can't be so highbrow. Late romantic music. That's a good fit here. And perhaps some songs. And poetry readings. After all, Quasimodo was Sicilian. Ungaretti. Montale. Luzi. Read by actresses with tremolo in their voices.'

6.

San Giovanni Battista, the roofless gothic church that I have been looking at from my terrace every day since I came here, with its rose window set slightly off-centre so that the whole façade has a mild squint, was in the early middle ages the site of Ortigia's synagogue. Not without reason is the entire quarter around Piazza del Precursore called *la Giudecca*, the Jewish quarter. Beneath the marble plaques bearing the names of streets and squares in Italian, a citizens' action group has fixed additional plaques bearing the Hebrew names. Thus we learn that around 1400, Via Minniti was called Ruga della Meschita, Via Alagona was Platea Vechiá, what more recently has been Vicolo della Giudecca was Ruga delli Bagni and Piazza del Precursore was Gía Platea Parva. For decades there was a fierce controversy as to whether the synagogue was really situated here, more or less on the ground where the Chiesa San Giovanni Battista stands today, or had not in fact once risen on the site of today's Chiesa di San Filippo Apostolo. A courageous activist named Anna Daniele di Bagni, who also uncovered the Hebrew baths that had been entirely buried eighteen metres beneath Via Alagona and made them accessible again, one day found a stone tablet in the apse of San Giovanni with a Hebrew inscription, which no one before her had noticed. The inscription mentions the synagogue of Siracusa, 'founded on law and faith'. A little later she found a further inscription, which talks of the donation of the land for the synagogue.

Of Jewish life in Ortigia we have no clear image. We only know that at the beginning of 1492 it came to a precipitous end. An edict from Isabella of Castile and Ferdinand of Aragon required the expulsion of the Jews from every territory of the Spanish crown, which included Sicily. Overnight, the Jewish families had to leave Ortigia, Syracuse, and every other Sicilian city. The Spanish authorities behaved like ruthless colonial overlords. They confiscated Jewish property and tore down their buildings or built on top of them. Almost nothing from this period survives and what does has been made unrecognisable. For example, not far from my apartment there was a publicly accessible space at ground level with a municipal water fountain. The outlines of a medieval Jewish shop were still clearly discernible: the entrance, the window display, the counter, over which goods were handed to customers on the street. Two years ago the façade was broken open and the walls were covered with giant vending machines, bathed in glaring neon light. The city government proved once again that it hands out permits without rhyme or reason.

Many of the buildings in la Giudecca have undergone transformations but have been able to preserve their outward appearance. Among these I count the Chiesa San Giovanni Battista, especially since its deconsecration in 1865, which then served as a quarantine station and a military barracks; later a coal store, a timber depot, a rubbish dump, and then again a storehouse for coal. In 1959, INDA, the organisation that organises the performances of classical plays at the Greek Theatre, took the church interior into its care, cleaned it out, and used it for concerts and small-scale theatre pieces. Later still the church served as the performance space for the *Teatro dei Pupi*, until the nearby church of San Filippo took it over again. Today very occasional church services are held there, framed with tentative, impure choral singing. But the *chiesa* has also developed into a favourite spot for weddings. From the beginning of May to the end of September, people get married there almost every day and the church rakes in some healthy hire charges. Weddings in southern European countries employ entire industries – from the floral decorations to the elaborate, eight-metre-long bridal veils, from the rented Bentley with whitewall tyres to the photographer with the latest drone equipment. The families of bride and groom, who parade together in their festive outfits in front of the church door, are in most cases ruining themselves financially to a disastrous extent and are trying to curb the sweat on their foreheads and necks with fans and enjoy the happy noise in spite of everything. Although fundamentally, you can see in their faces, they are waiting impatiently for the endless ceremony and their relatives' wordy good wishes to end.

7.

Caravaggio arrived in Syracuse in 1608. He was thirty-seven years old and a hunted man, a fugitive from Malta. Two powerful institutions were on his tail, the Vatican and the Order of St John. What had happened?

One of his early biographers, Giovanni Bellori, in his 1672 work *Vita di Michelangelo Merisi da Caravaggio*, cites a 'quarrel with a most noble knight' as the cause of his incarceration in Malta, but with few specifics. We know from many sources that Caravaggio was a hot-tempered hooligan who happily got into duels during his night-time boozing and never quite knew when enough was enough. The pope had already condemned him to death in Rome for his part in a brawl. Influential friends had wangled him an invitation to Malta from the Order of St John. He reached the island in July 1607. At first things shaped up well. The grand master of the Order, Alof de Wignacourt, was so enthralled by both the artist and his work that he had him paint his portrait and, after arduous negotiations, gained permission from the Vatican to make him a knight of the Order. But then there was a falling out with one of his brothers in the Order. The old pattern: Caravaggio severely injured this *cavaliere* and was arrested and thrown into a heavily guarded dungeon in Fort St Angelo. How he was able to escape this high-security facility and in the very same night find a ship bound for Sicily remains mysterious. Naïve Bellori reckons that the painter 'climbed over the prison walls and fled unrecognised at such speed that no one could catch up with him.' The crestfallen Wignacourt stripped Caravaggio of his knighthood. In Syracuse, an old acquaintance from his Roman days, the painter Mario Minniti, helped him out, offering him a place to stay and establishing connections for him with the city's senate. Ultimately the senate commissioned Caravaggio to paint an altarpiece for the recently restored church of Santa Lucia al Sepolcro, an image that was to have the burial of the city's patron saint as its theme.

It became a mighty painting, three metres wide and over four metres tall. In a high vault, probably a depiction of the catacombs under Chiesa Santa Lucia, we see a gloomy scene dominated by two giant gravediggers. The saint lies on the ground. She is small and delicate, a corpse, a human being. She is so slender against the heavy, muscular bodies of the two men, who have just begun to excavate her grave with their shovels. Caravaggio's manipulation of light is masterly. He spares no effect that might heighten the drama of the situation, even adding a whorl of light on the saint's small, white nose. Caravaggio wanted to awaken our empathy for this abused figure, to force the viewer's respect for her tormented body. On the neck of the corpse, we see the cut from the dagger's blow, one of the many tortures she endured.

I was disappointed the first time I saw this picture. I didn't like it. I had expected something else, something less depressing. Only gradually did I understand that for Caravaggio this was not about the glorious martyr. He wanted to capture the oppressive reality of a burial at which the gravediggers are the principal players. Their powerful arms and legs form an almost perfect circle around the woman lying on the ground. I join the ranks of the crowd of mourners, who form a second circle, a semi-circle around the dead woman. Among them is the bishop with a pointed mitre and a young, handsome priest, his shoulders covered by a long, blood-red stole. He is the only one who gazes steadfastly down at Lucia and so guides my gaze to her also.

8.

Most people who come here, who don't know anyone and don't want to move on immediately, will stay in a hotel. Before I was able to move into my apartment on Piazza del Precursore and before that, when I was looking for an apartment, I spent the night in a variety of Syracuse's hotels: most often the Hôtel des Étrangers next to Fonte Aretusa, which is mentioned in my 1934 *Baedeker* and lures you with its glorious view over the Porto Grande; and then at the pale-blue-painted Hotel Gutkowski, with its Polish name which seems so completely out of place in Ortigia; and the Grand Hotel Villa Politi, once the premier hotel on the square and now an elderly lady with a few wrinkles.

Maria Teresa Laudien, an Austrian aristocrat, commissioned the building of the Villa Politi in 1862 after meeting the love of her life, the painter Salvatore Politi, in Syracuse. With its position on the edge of the steeply sloped Latomia dei Cappucini and its fabulous view over the jagged coastline as far as Ortigia, it quickly became known beyond Italy's borders and grew into a meeting place of politicians, artists, and European aristocracy. The imposing building, initially intended as the residence of the Politi family, rapidly mutated into a luxury hotel. Winston Churchill stayed here, first during the Allied invasion of 1944 and then again in April 1955. Reputedly he declared: 'I never slept so well in my life' – a line the hotel uses in its marketing to this day. Other famous guests include the writers Gabriele d'Annunzio and Edmondo de Amicis, who excitedly reported in his diary of 1906 the delightful hours he had spent on the terrace of the Grand Hotel above the ancient Greek quarries. Over a century later, the film crew of director Giuseppe Tornatore and the ravishing Monica Bellucci, star of the film they were making, *Malena*, darted about between the columns that line the terrace. She slept at the hotel during shooting. Old postcards show a driveway of grand carriages, the foyer with its very weighty columns, and the opulence of the dining rooms, decorated in 'Liberty Style', an Italian variant of Art Nouveau.

The name derived from the Liberty department store in London, which specialised in fabrics and porcelain from the Far East and back then dictated what was considered *le dernier cri*, even in Syracuse.

Today the Politi is fighting for its life. Its once fantastic location is no more; the views out over the sea and Ortigia have been obstructed by dull apartment blocks from the 1970s and 1980s. The area around the Capuchin monastery has lost its allure. The action has moved to Corso Umberto and Ortigia. All the same, I visit the terrace of the Politi from time to time and conjure up Italo Svevo sitting next to me in his white straw hat. But however many negronis I order, they won't be able to save the Politi in the long run.

A noblewoman plays a role in the history of the Hotel Gutkowski as well. In this case, a Sicilian aristocrat, *la Marquesa*, who is still a frequent topic of discussion on account of her wealth and her lifestyle. She owned vast estates in Cassibile and Avola and near Catania. And it was said, behind closed doors (even, so Dora tells me, at her school run by nuns), that she was not averse to libertinism. A freethinker. Her predilection for deep-red and violet plush fabrics proved as much. In the Sicily of a century ago, red velvet was actually associated with frivolity and corruption. This spirited *marquesa* met a Polish officer named Gutkowski. She fell in love with him and gave the male entourage that had been sashaying around her their marching orders. It was her granddaughter, Paola, an agile, attractive, nervy character, who founded the hotel and runs it with an openness to new ideas. She got the Berlin designer Herbert Weinand, who had settled near Mount Etna many years earlier, to design tables and shelving for the hotel. From Militello, a small, baroque town near Catania, she brought a young and talented chef, who knows how to magic up remarkable gastronomic delights from strictly local produce night after night.

9.

Vincenzo Consolo, by contrast, provides the pleasures of the spirit. This Sicilian writer, a friend of Leonardo Sciascia and Gesualdo Bufalino, became known in Germany principally for his novels *The Wound of April* and *The Smile of the Unknown Mariner*, only to fall back into obscurity soon afterwards. In the last few days I have read *The Stones of Pantalica* for a second time. This volume gathers stories and reportage mainly written in the 1980s, when Sicily really was Italy's neglected backyard and in Palermo the Mafia were unleashing one appalling bloodbath after another.

Consolo's stories deal with the decline of the Sicily of the Greeks, the destruction of the environment, the exploitation of the peasants and workers, the suppression of their uprisings, and many another bleak topic. What binds these tales together is Consolo's language, his acute feeling for the tenderness and sensuousness of words, for startling constructions, for lyrical upswings, for unconventional syntax that can jolt us from our course. Two passages particularly impressed me.

One describes the quarries in Cusa, where huge blocks were hewn from the tufa and worked into drums for the columns of the Doric temples in Selinunte. The distance from the the Cava di Cusa to the temple precincts is about ten kilometres. In Cusa, because an earthquake or enemy attack put a stop to the work on the temples, colossal drums lie around among age-old olive trees, like glacial erratics, like the ungathered toys of giants.

The other passage is about Syracuse. Consolo recalls his very first visit there in 1950, when he attended a performance at the Greek Theatre of Euripides' *Iphigenia in Tauris* (a play he later translated into Italian with the Greek scholar Dario Del Corno):

A high-school student in a village in the Messina area called Barcellona, I was taken with my classmates to see some classical plays. That year they were performing the *Bacchae* by Euripides and *The Persians* by Aeschylus. I remember that my attention, my emotion, were not for the tragedies but for Syracuse: it seemed to me an exceptionally beautiful city. And not for its Greek antiquities, or at least not only for those, but also for its medieval and baroque architecture, for its modern *palazzi*, for its life, its atmosphere, its particular grace, its culture.

And Consolo continues:

I remember how, out of one of those desires that teenagers often feel, expressed as firm resolutions of things we might actually achieve, I solemnly told myself that when I was a 'grown-up' I would move to Syracuse and spend my entire life in this city.

That was in 1950. Thirty years later his love had cooled to the point of extinction. Consolo found the city coarse, almost barbarous. As he leaves the Greek Theatre he perceives nothing but misery and destruction:

> The oil refineries and chemical plants at Melilli and Priolo on the outskirts of Syracuse have corroded and poisoned the city. In the historic centre, on the island of Ortigia, the spectacle is even more depressing. The wondrous medieval, renaissance, baroque city, the city of the nineteenth and early twentieth century, is entirely degraded: a rotten, putrefied city. The Syracuse that I saw thirty years ago, the city I thought of going to live in, no longer exists.

Consolo is so heartbroken that he hopes, by invoking the names of all the streets, squares, palazzi, all the people he knows, the cafés and *trattorie*, that he may conjure up the return of 'his' Syracuse.

And today, another forty years on? The quail island has transformed again. Ortigia is no longer so neglected as Consolo described it for us. Older buildings have been painstakingly restored and parts of the Giudecca gentrified. And, besides, no one can withstand the magic of the gently curving cathedral square and the harbour promenades and the views out over the sea. Even for me, having lived here a long time now, some of the alleyways and squares seem almost too 'picturesque'. The poverty, scabbiness, and ruin that Consolo describes, and which still surface in Dora's memories of her school days, remain today only in Graziella, the quarter behind the old Bourbon prison, where the migrants and the poorest fishermen and craftsmen live. If schoolboy Consolo were to come to Syracuse today, he would, I am sure, resolve once more to spend his whole life in this city.

10.

When I arrived on Ortigia, six years ago now, the Quail Island was a Cat Island. There were cats everywhere. They lolled about on hot car rooves, slept in clay pots between scarred prickly pears, guarded the back entrance of the archbishop's palazzo, zigzagged through traffic, or played their indestructibly elegant games in the fenced-off precinct of Apollo's Temple.

One day, as I arrive again from Berlin to stay for a while on Piazza del Precursore, something in the cityscape strikes me. There are no cats. Not anywhere. As if the earth had swallowed them. I begin to look for them, go to the places where I've always encountered them. But my search is in vain. I ask Monteleone, Dora, Signora Ricutto, a vet whose surgery I walk past every day, our estate agent. Maddeningly, I never receive a clear answer. Or I get something disingenuous: 'Are there really no more cats? I'm sure I saw one yesterday.' 'An epidemic maybe? Or too much rat poison?' 'You'll only have to wait a little while. They breed so quickly.'

Why so shy to call things by their names? Why hide behind the city authorities, who, it was clear to me, had carried out a mass murder? The most absurd explanation came from my neighbour, Monteleone. A large circus had pitched its tent on the outskirts of the city, he said, and the circus folk had gathered up all the cats at night because they needed meat for their hungry lions. The only cat that remains is made of stone, a heraldic cat in a circular coat of arms over the entrance to Cortile Vega on Via della Maestranza. It smiles sadly down on the street, its ears pricked. It smiles sadly at the debates in the city's parliament: 'How do we get this plague under control?' asks one. 'How would a sterilisation programme look?' 'We need to take all the cats off the street and into safe custody.' 'But what does that mean, you cynic?' responds another. 'Into death?'

After a few days I discover on the site of some ruins two cats that have evidently survived the massacre. They are being cared for by Mariella, who feeds and tends to the survivors. Most often, she comes up to me on Via Logoteta with a rustling bag of dry pet food under her arm. She has unkempt hair, dark teeth, a tatty jacket of indistinct hue and a soft heart.

Gradually I learn that Mariella comes from a humble background, that her father worked on the land, but she did so well at the village school that the teacher put her forward for the lyceum. Two things stand out about her: her eyes, wide awake in spite of her age, sparkling even, and the glittering ring on the middle finger of her left hand. Its gold clasps a small gem of dark carnelian, engraved with a dolphin. The dolphin is hard to make out, but when light falls on it, the body and fins shine briefly and make a link to Arethusa. What Mariella lives on, no one knows. Behind the town hall, near the remains of the Ionic temple, she has set up a sort of cat garden, with sleeping areas, drinking bowls, and places for food. On some evenings before the massacre, a dozen cats frolicked here. Now there are two, and later three.

After a few weeks another cat woman emerges, a white-haired gnome on Via della Giudecca escorted by two cats that behave like dogs, with a wholly un-catlike devotion. One of these dog-cats is ginger, the other fluffed up and tri-coloured with a broad black mask around both eyes, which gives it a Zorro look. Simply adorable. And the ginger cat reminds me of a saying I have often heard here: 'Red coat, wicked coat.' Because ginger cats are supposed to bring bad luck.

11.

Over the years, I've bought up an assortment of old post-cards of Syracuse and its environs. One of these postcards shows two columns from the Temple of Olympian Zeus, which was built at the same time as the Temple of Apollo on Ortigia – that is, in the fifth century BC – and lies around three kilometres from the island, across the Porto Grande and near the rivers Anapo and Ciane. The temple must have been gigantic, with six columns on its shorter sides and seventeen on the longer. Of this colossus only two stumps of columns and some ashlars of the base remain. On the postcard, a small walking party have made themselves comfortable on the ashlars. Two men in formal black suits are chatting with a lady in a long winter coat, her dog beside her. It must be autumn or even winter. The trees have lost their leaves. One man pours something from a carafe into a glass for the other. Even with my magnifying glass, I can't make out what it is: Wine? A liqueur? Or plain water?

I have repeatedly tried to visit these columns and failed every time. This time too, the gate of the gravel road is shut with an iron chain. There are thorny bushes and impassable terrain to the left and right. I resolve to walk down along the Ciane and slog through the tall grass until I reach a plateau a little higher up. I drink in the smells of the grass. A beautiful green lizard stands motionless with summer's drowsiness. When I finally make it to the two columns, several wall lizards have anchored themselves to the porous stone with their long claws. I imagine that their shrewd black pin eyes follow me as I move. I have brought a few ripe apricots with me from the market in a paper bag. The smell of the fruit draws them in and I manage to entice one slender lizard onto the palm of my hand. It plucks vigorously at the orange-yellow flesh of the fruit. This I find far more exciting than the two dead columns.

One from the Rock

1.

Only on thoroughly grey winter days can Ortigia look shabby. Then the façades show their grey mould. Cracks and fungus everywhere. The moss advances. Rotten rooves on rotted houses. A damp gossamer in the air, which goes well with the faded black of the priest's soutane. Everything is coated with an inexplicable black-silvery patina, such as only southern Italy can conjure. In the suburbs it gets properly grim. So many workshops, gyms, cheap Asian supermarkets, tyre fitters, stonemasons selling ghastly sculptures for gardens and parks, with a funeral parlour and the El Sole bar in between. Then a negroni is the only consolation. On the table at the Station Bar it glows like a furnace with ice cubes. At a distance it looks like the low winter sun. The walk back to Ortigia, along Corso Umberto in the damp of evening and across the bridge onto the island, which stands entirely on stone and is made of stone, makes the ships look even slower than in the morning. 'He's from the rock,' people in the new town say of someone who lives on Ortigia. I am from the rock. Because the margins disappoint and dissatisfy, I must walk into the old centre, to the rock, to the stone.

2.

One cheerful afternoon, as we were sat in Caffè Minerva and when I was absolutely no longer expecting it, the Baron invited me to his palazzo.

The next day, I am standing at the entrance. He opens the tall, wrought-iron gates himself. I had expected a domestic servant. As ever, he looks very dapper, wearing a waistcoat of yellow corduroy that goes well with his pleated dark-brown neck scarf and conceals his slight, firm embonpoint. He leads me up the outside staircase, we walk through his private chapel – too heavily restored, for my taste – and arrive into a high, rectangular hall. Stuffed antelope heads stare down at us from pale-green walls.

'I didn't know you were a hunter.'

'In my youth. In my youth,' he repeats. 'That's all over now.'

He strides towards a piano, which stands in one corner of the hall next to an extensive area of seating. On the black mirror of the piano lid stand the inevitable family photos in ornate silver frames. The strength of the sunlight has faded the images to the point of unrecognisability. Regardless, Lucio Tasca di Lignari takes the time to gently wipe over the glass of some with his corduroy sleeve and show me his mother on a dressage horse among a swarm of children; in another photo, she sits alone and beautifully posed on a garden bench with an elegiac expression. The figure is almost white around its edges; it reminds me of Man Ray's solarised portraits. A white merging into age-old yellow.

'Doesn't she look like Lady Hamilton?' says Lucio with studied exuberance. 'Of course you know she lived here briefly with her husband Lord Hamilton, right nearby, in Palazzo Beneventano by the cathedral. And Admiral Nelson came to visit her. A "threesome"', he adds in English. He opens his arms and chuckles.

In one of these bleached-out photographs I can see the Baron himself, wearing a diving suit. He is hugging a mussel-encrusted amphora. One foot rests on an oxygen cylinder lying on the ground, as if it were an animal he had just slain.

'After hunting, I had a passion for archaeology, underwater research in particular. I took diving courses and sought out an East German archaeologist called Gerhard Kapitän. The craziest twist of fate. He was on a trip to Italy in 1961 when the Wall was built, decided not to return to East Berlin, and settled in Syracuse instead.' He points at the amphora in the photograph. 'Kapitän could tell you about amphorae for hours at a time. He had a mania for research. Very well-known academically. There's even a kind of late Roman amphora named after him.'

I've heard this name, Gerhard Kapitän, somewhere before, but I cannot place it. Lucio tells me that he died here in Syracuse in 2011, so I can't have met him in person, as I didn't move into my home here in Ortigia until spring 2015.

'Perhaps you heard his name in connection with the famous wreck off Marzamemi. He was involved in salvaging and sifting through all the material found on the ship. It was one of his outstanding achievements. He was much acclaimed for it.'

After a respectful pause, he continues: 'Come on – now I'll show you *my* finds.' He leads me into a kind of *studiolo* with glass-fronted cabinets, vitrines, and beautiful shelves of a reddish wood reaching up to the ceiling. Everywhere is crammed with glass vases, clay jugs, sherds, fragments of a marble frieze, oil lamps, statuettes, arrowheads. There is a badly battered *kouros* too, which plainly must have spent more than two millennia in saltwater. A large stone anchor leans in one corner.

'The anchor was given me by a colleague, who was renowned for her collection of stone anchors. She was called Honor Frost, a British woman who was born in Nicosia, when Cyprus was still a British Crown Colony. She was the real pioneer of underwater archaeology, a model for all of us, even Gerhard Kapitän. For me too, though I really wasn't playing in the same league. I was, and am, an amateur.'

He paces along the shelves, expounds on the form of the iridescent lachrymatories, which originate from Marsala, then returns once again to the anchor.

'It's crazy, the things people collect. Honor wasn't just an expert on ancient shipbuilding. She was the world-wide expert on the classification of stone anchors as well. This one here is truly dear to me,' he sighs. 'Only it is very cumbersome.'

The Baron notes that his antique cabinet of curiosities is not failing to have an effect on me. In truth, this jumble of beauty and brokenness has struck me hard.

'The least cumbersome part of my collection,' he goes on,

'as well as the most attractive, is of course the coins. But, as I already told you, they're in the country. Hidden away at my winery. You must come there as well some time. As a foretaste, I will now serve you a *Moscato di Siracusa*.'

He opens a small cupboard, against which the kouros is leaning, and extracts a bottle of Muscat and two glasses. 'We cultivate this grape variety there. In the foothills of my beloved Hyblaean Mountains.'

'*Cincin!*'

'*Saluti!*'

'Pretty intense!'

'Yes, a little like the Sauternes that the French serve with *foie gras*.'

3.

At midday the sun breaks through the clouds and lays a wide band of saffron across the sea. The colour of the Palazzo Russo recalls the thin white layer of sugar that forms on the surface of honey in a jar. At the entrance to the farmers' market there are tall, slanted stands of chestnuts from Etna: shimmering brown cascades, beautiful to look at. Back to the cathedral square. The way it bulges out towards the Porto Grande becomes especially clear in the afternoon light, a gently curving semicircle that reminds me afresh of the belly of a great ship. Maybe the baroque city planners actually intended it – the cathedral square as a cross section of a magnificent white ship, with the cathedral side as the deck and the convex side as the keel?

The musician is back on the square today. He plays a bruised, old accordion, but that doesn't help matters. His hair is dishevelled, his face bewildered. The way he stands there reminds me of a painting by István Farkas called *The Fool of Syracuse*, which hangs in a prominent position in the National Gallery in Budapest. In the centre of this image, painted by Farkas in 1930, stands a man in a pale suit on a white track. He has a strikingly thick, reddish beard and a broad-brimmed hat. I remember all this, and how the horizon of black sea curves across the picture. This sea with its long, black tongue shoves its way in between a withered ochre landscape and a dirty, pinkish volcano. Etna, with its pall of smoke.

The fool in the picture plays no instrument. His left arm is raised, as if he wants to summon something that comes from the sea. In his right hand he holds a toothed rod, like a sceptre or weapon or magic wand. It could also be the long, saw-like rostrum of a sawfish, the tapering point of its elongated, shark-like body. On each side of this rostrum, which begins immediately in front of the fish's eyes, stand between fourteen and twenty-three teeth, closer and closer together towards the tip. I decide that the fool is swinging the jagged sword of a sawfish in his right hand.

To the left of the man we see a house with a black dog sitting in front of it. The first – and only – time I saw this picture in Budapest, I thought that the fool was Van Gogh, not in the sweltering heat of Arles, but in the brutal August heat of Syracuse. There are pictures by Francis Bacon which show the done-for Van Gogh on a Provençal country road, his easel strapped to his back. Here Van Gogh has metamorphosed into the madman of Syracuse.

4.

The grave of Count August von Platen was difficult to find. I knew only that it was located in the gardens of the villa of Count Landolina.

Landolina was a major figure in the Syracuse of the nineteenth century. He belonged to the wealthy nobility, was a patron of the arts and earned great kudos as an archaeologist for his research into the city's history. It was he who unearthed that plump Aphrodite, also known as the 'Venus Landolina', for which Guy de Maupassant travelled from Paris to Syracuse. She was not really pretty. She had thick fetlocks and her knees were too round. Ferdinand Gregorovius describes her in his inimitable style: 'The body is very full, the lower body strikingly strong and powerful; a Venus for Michelangelo. Among all the famous figures of the goddess of love, from Milos, from Capua, from the Capitol in Rome, from Florence, the Syracusan stands out least in allure and most in its full womanly beauty. Her movement has nothing of the coquettish grace of the Venuses of Florence or Rome. She is more at rest in the fullness of her divine sensuality.' Be that as it may, the dimples of this half-naked woman – she has gathered drapery over her private parts – incited the French writer to several cries of pleasure on paper. Today she is the showpiece of the new Archaeological Museum, a hexagonal concrete octopus set into the gardens of Villa Landolina, after the museum on the cathedral square grew too small.

When August von Platen came to Syracuse in November 1835, fleeing the cholera, the Venus as yet lay deep and unknown in the earth. Platen was ailing. Count Landolina risked himself to look after him and assigned two of his servants to nurse him around the clock. But the poet died of internal bleeding only a short time afterwards, on 5 December 1835.

At that time there was no cemetery in Syracuse that accepted protestants. Landolina took pleasure in laying out a small collection of non-Catholic graves within his grounds. The Franconian poet was, for him, a welcome addition. As late as 1968, one Italian travel guide still referred to it as *'il romantico cimitero dei Protestanti'*. The cemetery, hidden away between a quarry and the wall of the villa gardens, was not open to the public. The first time I enquired after the site of Platen's grave, a man at the entrance gate to the villa gardens, who was also selling tickets for the museum, gruffly repelled me. The path there had not been made safe, he said, and there was a risk of landslips, so access was forbidden. 'Perhaps next year it will be possible again,' he pronounced. A familiar situation for me. I have many times failed in my attempts to find the tombs of the famous. In the San Michele cemetery in Venice I searched for hours in vain for the grave of Ezra Pound. Later I wanted to visit my friend Luigi Nono in the same cemetery. He had just recently been interred. At least the custodian of the graveyard knew who Nono was. He handed me a leaflet for visitors with the layout of the cemetery printed on it, and made a dot with a thick, black marker pen in *Recinto IV*: 'Here he rests. A great son of the city.'

Only at my third attempt did I manage to outfox the staff at the entrance to the Archaeological Museum and gain access to the rear section of the gardens. The unpaved path was completely overgrown and led up a hill. I was on the point of giving up my quest when I discovered a small patch of ground with four graves, directly in front of the wall of rock which also forms the perimeter of the grounds. One gravestone for an American man shows a female mourner in half relief, crowned with cypress and weeping over an urn. Next to it, the modest grave of an Englishwoman. For Platen, Landolina had a memorial of polychromatic marble inserted in 1836 into the natural rock face. But this was not enough for the poet's devotees from Munich and his native town of Ansbach. They commissioned a sort of obelisk, a square stele that tapers as it rises and is crowned with a larger-than-life-sized bust of the poet. When I first caught sight of this stele among the whip-thin cypresses with the high, drone buzz of cicadas all around, I was reminded of the familiar opening two lines of von Platen's 'Tristan':

Who has beheld Beauty with his eyes
Has already entrusted himself to Death

In Germany, hardly anyone knows von Platen any more. A few songs, two or three ghazals, his feud with Heine, his affirmation of same-sex love. He almost seems more present in Syracuse than he is among us Germans. In the ticket office of Castello Maniace a book is on display containing a selection of his poems translated into Italian. The Palermo-based publisher Sellerio has released a long essay by Pino Di Silvestro on the poet's death in Syracuse. And the wide street that runs northwards from Viale Teocrito past the Villa Landolina is still called Via Augusto von Platen.

The funeral procession must have passed along this road on 6 December 1835. Heinrich Wilhelm Schulz, an art historian who had introduced Platen in Naples to his Italian colleague, Giacomo Leopardi, sent the Countess von Platen, the poet's mother, a long account of the final days and burial of her son: four black-clad pages processed on the four sides of the 'state carriage' bearing the coffin, which was covered with a brocade cloth, he wrote. Two further pages sat alongside the coffin; two coaches and several friends on foot followed. 'A numberless crowd, full of pity, enveloped the funeral procession' – thus Schulz concluded his report. Was it like this? Or was it base gawking, with no interest in who was being borne to their grave? Or was Schulz exaggerating, to comfort the mother? Today, almost two hundred years later, lorries thunder along Via Augusto von Platen and drown out the cicadas and the memories.

5.

In Ortigia, many roads lead to the market. Most often I take Via della Maestranza as far as Piazza Archimede and then walk down Corso Matteoti to the Temple of Apollo, not without a stop-off at Caffè Viola, which reminds me of an old Shell petrol station in Berlin and offers the best and crispest *cornetto vuoto* in the city. From Piazza Archimede it's also possible to take Via Dione, which likewise leads down to the market. Finally, Via Vittorio Veneto, known in earlier times as *Mastra Rua*, runs parallel to the sea, past the old Bourbon prison to the other end of the market street, where Fratelli Burgio have set up their delicatessen temple.

Elio Vittorini's grandparents lived at number 140, *Mastra Rua*. When Elio was not travelling in the province with his father, an employee of the state railway, he lived here with a constantly changing line-up of members of his large family. A commemorative plaque is fixed to the façade of this modest, pink, thoroughly weather-beaten house:

> In this house on 23 July 1908 was born
> Elio Vittorini
> Champion of Liberty
> Hero of Italian Literature
> He honoured Syracuse, Italy, Culture
> The city remembers him on the 75th anniversary of his birth

How often have I read this plaque on my almost daily walk to the market! Mastra Rua, which was a major thoroughfare in medieval Ortigia, was destroyed, like all Ortigia, by the great earthquake of 1693, and then completely rebuilt shortly afterwards, with simple houses alongside small *palazzi*, fine examples of baroque architecture. And thus manual workers, the lower middle classes, and salaried employees like Elio's father lived cheek by jowl with minor nobility. In a short autobiography, composed by Elio Vittorini in 1949 'for my foreign readers', he considers the Syracuse of his childhood:

> Syracuse is a city of sailors and farm workers, built on a

small island, linked to Sicily by a long bridge. I was born here on 23rd July 1908 in a house from which, when I was seven years old, I saw a steamship full of Chinese people sink. Behind the house, bastions stretched out above the sea. A hundred metres further on there was a square where the farmers who lived in our neighbourhood set down their carts in the evening after a long day's work. Their animals – mules, donkeys and horses – followed them homewards and slept there from seven o'clock in the evening to three in the morning, when they would go back to work. In every house there was a small inner courtyard with a wooden pen for the animals and a stone washtub. The men, who came home in the evenings with their animals, and the women, who washed the laundry in the trough in the courtyard, were my relations on my mother's side: uncles, aunts and cousins. Of my relations on my father's side I knew little. About them there were only stories, because they were sailors. My father was employed by the railway. We only lived in the house in Syracuse when he had a vacation or had been able to take time off from his duties. The rest of the year we spent in small railway station buildings with barred windows and wasteland all around us.

Literature offered him solace and distraction. *Robinson Crusoe* and *The Thousand and One Nights* were favourite books. With his sister and two brothers he re-enacted scenes purportedly from these books, mostly on the platforms of train stations. Much later, as a young man, Elio met Rosa, sister of the poet Salvatore Quasimodo, at

Syracuse station. I have already mentioned the plaque at the station entrance which commemorates this 'event'. The two became engaged. Syracusans love to repeat a story about them, that the hotel refused to accommodate an unmarried couple, and so they spent their first night together at the Greek Theatre, under the starry sky. In her memoirs, Rosa spills not a word on the subject.

Elio soon moved away from Syracuse. In 1928 he went to Florence and later to Milan. Syracuse surfaces only sporadically in his work, though it's true that his novel *The Red Carnation* describes Piazza Duomo on its first page. And his best-known book, *Conversations in Sicily*, with a rhythm and terse sentences that make the language sway, reads like a railway journey to a symbolic destination, Syracuse.

Vittorini came once more to Syracuse, in 1943. The city was living in fear of Allied bombardment. The catacombs of Santa Lucia and San Giovanni and the sprawling underground vaults beneath the cathedral square, with their passageways ramifying down as far as the great harbour, served as air-raid shelters. Vittorini had come to recruit old friends for the resistance. But his former comrades disappointed him. They had become functionaries, who had adapted to or, even worse, sympathised with Mussolini. After a few days he returned despondently to Milan.

Syracuse and a broad swathe of Sicily were heavily damaged by bombing. The population was battered and frightened. Documentary photos of the time show men, women, and children densely crowded into the hypogeum under the cathedral. We lack literary witnesses to put alongside these oppressive images. I know only of the diary entries of Hanns Cibulka, who was in Sicily in 1943 as a twenty-three-year-old signalman in the German army. He writes of battles and air raid warnings, of low-flying Spitfires and four-engined British and American bombers, which had set out from Bizerte in Tunisia. 'Under the roar of the engines the sky shatters into loud blue pieces.' As he hangs his signals cables over olive trees and lays them through lemon groves, so that the command posts of the German troops can communicate with each other, he also time and again describes the Sicilian landscape in his characteristically clear and succinct language. The cables are vulnerable: animals gnaw at them and shrapnel strikes them. Cibulka ranges across the maquis, and, without meaning to, sings the praises of the flora on Etna's slopes. In the same precise language he captures the absurdity of this war, of every war. After the start of 'Operation Husky', as the Allied invasion of southern Italy was called, he sees tens of thousands of young soldiers confronting each other, not knowing why they were supposed to kill each other. Combat operations in Sicily lasted thirty-eight days in all. 855,000 soldiers faced each other: 405,000 Italians and Germans, 450,000 British and Americans. Cibulka published his Sicilian journals, a very long time afterwards, in East Germany under the title *Night Watch*. His descriptions can be piercing. Weeks later, long after I had put aside his slender book of memories, the sounds of the fighter bombers and the machine guns would not leave me, nor the night's heavy silence that followed, in which rumours about progress at the front spread unchecked.

6.

I first visited the catacombs under Basilica di Santa Lucia al Sepolcro in the new town soon after my arrival. Now, a few years later, I want to return to the Borgata district and test my memories. The basilica stands on the open side of Piazza Santa Lucia, a very large rectangle defined by doubled rows of trees. In my memory this square is a metaphysical place, almost paralysed by silence, hemmed in by melancholic two-storey houses. Today it is exactly as it was on my first visit. Old men sit taciturn on a bench. Two children play noiselessly with a ball. The few passersby move in the half-shade like dolls by de Chirico. Or like characters in a black-and-white film from the 1960s. A motorbike rattles past, then the silence closes back over the square like an enormous bell jar. The square tells the story of Lucia's death, her martyrdom. She was beheaded, so we are told, on the spot marked in the basilica by the granite column to the right of the sanctuary. Next to the basilica, the architect Giovanni Vermexio, who also built the town hall on Ortigia's cathedral square, built in 1629 an octagonal burial chapel, half sunk into the ground. Steps lead down to its entrance. The saint's burial chamber, like the rest of the catacombs, lies deep underground in the rock. Believers who wish to visit Lucia find themselves at the same level as her tomb; they need look neither up nor down. The recess in the limestone is empty, as empty as the great square outside. To help the visitor make the imaginative leap, a glass-fronted shrine has been installed in front of the altar that frames the open, rock-cut tomb. In it lies a Lucia of marble, half propped on a high pillow, her eyes closed, as pretty as a picture, lost and introverted. It was made by one Gregorio Tedeschi in 1634. An atrociously poor copy of the painting by Caravaggio hangs on the wall to the left of the altar. Confused, I climb back up the steps and then a little later discover the original as the central altarpiece in the basilica.

Knowing, as we do, that the Byzantine mercenary general George Maniakes took the saint's mortal remains in 1038 to Constantinople, where they were presented as a gift to the epileptic Emperor Michael IV, this burial chapel seems something of a paradox. Was the idea to worship a sepulchre by then already empty for half a millennium? Did they want to express in stone their hope that one day the relics would return to Syracuse? Return, incidentally, no longer from Constantinople but from Venice, since the Venetians had already plundered the mortal remains in 1204 and carried them back to the lagoon city. On the Grand Canal today you can still read the following inscription on the façade of Chiesa San Geremia: *'Lucia Vergine di Siracusa in questo tempio riposa. All'Italia e al Mondo ispiri luce e pace.'* In 1955 Angelo Roncalli, then patriarch of Venice, later Pope John XXIII, had the saint's face covered with a silver mask, to protect it from dust. Later the Vatican permitted a brief return of the relics to Syracuse, the city of her birth. But the eight-cornered funerary temple in Borgata stands, as it always has, over an empty grave. Perhaps that is why her devotees during the great procession in December shout so loudly *'Siracusaaaaana è'* – 'She is a Syracusan' – as if her absence might give rise to an especially strong feeling of belonging.

7.

This bone-hard island of rock surprises me often in the evenings with its soft, North African moods. This may have something to do with the fact that from my terrace I am mostly aware not of the city's Baroque redevelopment but of the beige and white cubes of its rooftop apartments, which in their tangled overlapping evoke the Orient. The Arab Syracuse. This thought has been running round my head ever since I discovered, entirely by chance, a spacious inner courtyard on Via della Amalfitania, a small street which runs from Via Cavour down to the great harbour. Named *Corte dei Bottai*, it had evidently been a courtyard of traders in bottles and served as a temporary depot for wine merchants. This *corte*, with its beautifully curved, partly covered passages and grandiose outside staircase, immediately made me think of a caravanserai, a 'hotel' from Syracuse's Arab period. But then I found a notice from the antiquities authorities, explaining that it belongs to a street network from Greek times, most of which still lies hidden under what is today Via Cavour. A layer – *una stratificazione* – almost 2,000 years old had been uncovered, testifying to something of the spatial thinking of an ancient city, a pattern of lines and volumes that, as you may read on the sign, influenced the structure of the city up into the Baroque period.

All the same, that image of the caravanserai, such as I've seen in small Syrian cities and in the Turkish part of Nicosia, stuck in my head. Fittingly, a few days after my discovery of the *Corte dei Bottai*, I find a letter in my letterbox from a Tunisian friend, the poet Khaled Najar. He writes to me that in the Tunis of his childhood there was '*beaucoup de Sicilie*' – a lot of Sicily. The house where Garibaldi found shelter in exile stands to this day on Rue de la Commission. The suburb of La Goulette, he writes, positively teemed with shops selling ricotta and pasta and pungently roasted *caffè* and *cannoli*. The best car mechanics in the city were Sicilians. In their workshops they made a weary Renault 4 into a Porsche. As I am reading Khaled's letter, many of my own memories return. I think of the Restaurant Tontonville, with its host, a scrawny cook from Messina. I had often eaten there with Khaled, among cheerful, homesick Sicilians.

The Arabisation driven by Habib Bourguiba, first president of post-Independence Tunisia, erased many Sicilian traces in Tunis after 1957. Businesses run by foreigners were harassed. Bullying officialdom choked the life out of the smaller companies, to the point where many Sicilians had no option but to return to their native island. The most prominent among them, Claudia Cardinale, who was born in La Goulette, went to Rome. There is a mirror image of this in Syracuse, where few concrete traces of the Arab presence remain, though admittedly, that was ten centuries ago. The architectural modifications from the cathedral's interval as a mosque were reversed later. Only in the apse are there some pathetic remnants of Arab–Byzantine mosaics. The ornamental quality of the cathedral's beautiful floors of multicoloured marble may remind you of Arab patterns, but they date from the fifteenth century. In summer, Marsala and Trapani on the south coast radiate a thoroughly Maghrebi flair, which Syracuse cannot match, even though I am ambushed, in certain arrangements of July light, by images of my childhood in Tunisia.

Dora tells me that the strongest traces of the Arab influence are in the kitchen, in Sicilian dishes. In the early Middle Ages, the Arabs brought not only citrus fruit, not only date palms to Sicily but also cinnamon, saffron, aniseed and nutmeg. The Greeks had lived frugally by comparison. The thoroughly refined cuisine that we recognise today only arrived with the Arabs. A highly developed Arabic poetics, some historians argue, emerged at the same time. This art of poetry was born one summer night in 827 AD, when a fleet landed at Mazara carrying Arabs, Berbers, Persians, Egyptians, and Maghrebis, who at first settled on the south coast. Here was the prelude to an extraordinary time shaped by a spirit of toleration between different ethnicities, cultures, peoples, and religions, not unlike the shared community of Andalusia in the same period. Not only Palermo, but also Catania and Syracuse became, little by little, cosmopolitan cities.

The Catania-born composer and singer Etta Scollo writes:

> When I visited the Zisa Palace in Palermo and listened to the hubbub of voices in the Ballarò market, I tried to pick out the notes of Arabic from the Sicilian. As I did so, the words of Leonardo Sciascia came into my head, that it was after the Arab conquest that the inhabitants of Sicily had begun to behave like Sicilians. But only with difficulty did I recognise the Palermo of al-Idrisi,

first geographer of the world, or the Syracuse of Ibn Hamdis, the famous Sicilian–Arab poet.

Etta Scollo has set poems by Ibn Hamdis to music and sung them in an uncannily affecting, even heartrending – I can think of no other word – way. Born in Syracuse in 1056, Ibn Hamdis died on Mallorca in 1133. His family was wealthy. They arrived in Sicily in the wake of the Arab conquest in the ninth century and settled in the Val di Noto. When the Normans took Messina in 1072, Ibn Hamdis had to flee to Sfax and then from Sfax to Seville, where for thirteen years he contributed to the blossoming of the art of poetry in *al-Andalus*. Many of his poems speak of his longing for Sicily:

> My Sicily. With every memory
> The hopeless pang returns.
> Youth. Again I see my lost happy follies,
> My wonderful friends.
> Oh Paradise, from which I was driven!
> What use, to recall your splendour?

Etta Scollo has sung this text as well. Ibn Hamdis lived at the end of this era of dialogue and exchange. His poems seem to me like the swansong of Arab Syracuse. A song of leave-taking, separation and loss.

8.

Syracuse has experienced many declines, suffered many losses. In the modern era, the lost significance of the harbour was decisive. The Syracusans slept through the ambitions of Catania and Palermo; when the maritime trade routes were being reorganised, they did not get involved. There is still the odd freighter that strays into the Porto Grande; there are the ferries to Malta; but fundamentally the city's sea traffic has collapsed and with it all the suppliers and associated businesses that are part of a harbour: the agents, financiers, warehousers, surveyors, chandlers, ship repairers, and insurers. All kaput.

The great harbour had a great past. Think of the fleets that anchored here and the mighty sea battles. Or think of the *Syracusia*, one of the largest freight and passenger transport ships in the ancient world. Designed by Archimedes, it was built in a dockyard near Syracuse around 240 BC by Archias of Corinth, on the orders of the tyrant Hieron II. According to an account by the historian Moschion of Phaselis, the *Syracusia* could transport up to 1,800 tonnes and around 1,900 passengers, as well as 200 soldiers and a gigantic catapult, devised by Archimedes. The exact dimensions of the ship are unknown. Michael Lahanas, a modern-day researcher into the ancient world, conjectures that she was 55 metres long, 14 metres wide and 13 metres tall. Too 'corpulent', at any rate, for a Sicilian harbour to be able to accommodate her. Thus she sailed on her sole voyage, from Syracuse to Alexandria, where she dropped anchor and later was made a gift to the ruler Ptolemy III Euergetes.

The ancient historians were writers of ample imagination, who wanted constantly to offer their readers something unheard of. But perhaps Athenaeus is not simply in the usual realm of exaggeration when he describes the ship's upper deck, supported by finely carved figures of Atlas and with eight towers standing upon it, each one manned by two archers and four warriors in full kit. Athenaeus also records the amenities the *Syracusia* had in readiness for its passengers. On the upper deck, apparently, there were leisure areas, a garden, and a canopied heated pool. While the lower decks were designated for the crew and soldiers, the middle deck housed a library – with a marble floor and ivory-adorned shelves for the scrolls – a gymnasium, and a small temple. The statue that was supposed to have stood in the temple has not, to this day, been identified. Was it Aphrodite or Amphitrite, the Nereid who was a consort of Poseidon? The scholars quarrel. Nothing is really documented. Is it all just intoxicated memory? In any case, this mega-ship is a thrilling spur for the imagination. It won't let me go. Sometimes the urge seizes me to embark on a grand library tour, to find out more about this giant ship, the *Titanic* of its time.

In summer, when the supersized yachts of Russian or Greek oligarchs moor at the quay of the Porto Grande, it is the image of the *Syracusia* that rises before my eyes. What became of her, no one knows. In Alexandria, the son of Ptolemy III attempted to outdo the *Syracusia* and ordered the building of a gigantic warship. The *Tessarakonteres* was meant to be able to accommodate 4,000 oarsmen and 2,850 soldiers. Plutarch mentions this crazed project but drily notes that the ship was incapable of movement, unfit for even the smallest manoeuvre.

9.

The day has arrived when Lucio will take me with him to his wine estate. It is early spring. As soon as we leave Syracuse's ugly industrial estates behind us, the orange and lemon groves begin on both sides of the road. The freshest green, gleaming as if polished. Then, shortly before Floridia, a small pine wood, blue-green needles. The rising hills are scattered with the farmsteads of landowners, defensive structures, limewashed the colour of rosewood or ochre. The arrangement of gate, steps, terraces, and windows seems casual but is thoroughly considered. Around the farmsteads are rows of prickly pear – living walls – or pieces of limestone boulder laid on top of each other without mortar. Beyond are the spring blossoms and above the blossoms the light in uproar.

The Baron's Rover effortlessly scales the first hills of the Hyblaean Mountains and then, in a valley, it is stretched out before us, his *masseria*. The two-storey main house in the centre is surrounded by extensive stables, forming a long rectangle around a tower that Lucio tells me was heavily fortified in the nineteenth century. Three old palms and a mighty, dark-purple, almost black bougainvillea leaning against the main house organise the inner courtyard. The proportions of the yard and the colour of the old stone warm the heart and give confidence in the world.

The Baron shows me the *cantina*, the wine cellar with its enormous aluminium tanks; the former stables, now converted into a hotel with six rooms and every amenity; then the kitchen and the main house. On the first storey, two doors lead out from the *salotto* onto a large terrace with an awning stretched over it, or rather a heavy canopy made of broad strips of deep yellow and joyful red fabric, lending an orange tinge to the whole ambiance. The floor of the terrace is glazed tile, laid in a blue and white zig-zag pattern, which forms a bold, wonderfully cool contrast to the warm colours of the canopy. The terrace is enclosed by a classical balustrade, which is to say by a long, orderly row of columns shaped like bowling pins. The handrail of the balustrade is covered with lichens and hard moss and seems even older and more mottled than the entire *masseria*, which has preserved a kind of seigneurial charm.

The Baron introduces me to the cook, the gardener, and the cellar master and his assistants, who look after the wine. 'It's a gruelling business,' he remarks. 'Too much competition.'

'And too much quality control,' adds the cellar master.

'But now I will lead you into the holy of holies. After all, we have to earn our *pranzo*.' We walk across the court-yard to the fortified tower. The Baron's *studiolo* is on the first floor. A large desk stands in the centre of the room. On the walls there are shelves of folios, atlases, and books bound in leather with red and blue labels on the spines. On a console table there are several teaching globes, black and mysterious. Lucio rummages awkwardly in his trouser pocket for a key, finally finds it and unlocks the uppermost drawer of the writing table. He pulls out several rectangular cases, lined with blue velvet. His coins are stored inside in circular recesses, like precious chocolates.

'I bought these cases in Vienna, in a shop near the Hofburg. They're very practical.' He shows me silver drachmas from Gela first, from around 400 BC. These coins are renowned for their exceptionally precise depictions of animals. There are sleek falcons with menacingly curved beaks and plump quails, but best of all are the crabs, portrayed with such exact detail that they seem alive, as if they might at any moment leave the narrow circle of the coin. With five legs on either side of the sculpted carapace, the powerful claws on the forelegs, and eyes like dark ball-head pins recessed into the armoured brow. In another case, Punic silver coins sparkle. They are instantly recognisable by their characteristic horse's head, palm tree, and round moon, symbol of the god Baal. The greatest attraction for me are the gold coins from Greece. One shows the head of Philip II, father of Alexander the Great, in profile. Lucio opens case after case. He has saved the tetradrachma, with Arethusa's head surrounded by four swimming dolphins, for last. 'We've already talked about these,' he says. 'They're considered the most beautiful coinage in the ancient world.'

He pulls out a magnifying glass. 'You see here,' he says. 'These engravers just knew how good they were, and so they began to sign their creations. This was around 415 BC. On the obverse you always see the victorious quadriga. Earlier, the horses were shown at a walk, then from this period, galloping. And on the reverse is the head of our revered nymph of the spring.'

He flicks on the desk lamp and lays out the coins directly under the beam of light. 'This coin was cut by two artists, the obverse by Euainetos and the reverse by Eumenes. Their signatures are clearly visible: Eumenes on the reverse directly below the truncation of her neck – can you see it? – and

Euainetos is on the tablet that Nike holds up in the air as she hovers over the quadriga.' Now he shows me more drachma, with Arethusa presented front on. 'Kimon was the first to create this frontal portrait. It was copied enthusiastically throughout the Greek cultural world. I don't know why. Myself, I would put the profile portrait way ahead of it.'

We hear a bell. 'Ah! That means lunch is ready.' Before we walk down, the Baron opens another door, which is set into the wall and barely noticeable. It leads into a further room. I see several telescopes on antediluvian stands and the disk of an astrolabe. 'That's my den. My playground for stargazing,' he says. 'But now we must go to the *salotto*.'

To begin, there is bruschetta with fresh ricotta. The cheese is laid on as thick as the slice of toasted and oil-drizzled bread. The cook has scattered pepper and lavender salt onto the ricotta. 'It's simple and delicious,' I enthuse. 'My compliments to the chef!' Lucio calls for her and she emerges from the kitchen, bringing the main course at the same time, a festively fragrant rack of lamb. Lucio asks her for a brief explanation of how the dish was prepared.

'The lamb is from the local area,' she says. 'I hung the meat for a short time, then seared it and coated it in a breadcrumb crust before putting it in the oven to roast. I mixed the breadcrumbs with chopped fennel, garlic, some parsley and more lavender, so that we can follow that familiar flavour through. I hope I've succeeded.'

A small feast. We do justice to the Nero d'Avola and follow the dark strips of light that the sun casts through the red-yellow canopy outside and onto our banquet.

10.

The *Teatro Greco* in the new town is the largest theatre in Sicily. The tyrant, Hieron II, extended it in 220 BC, so that it can hold 15,000 people. Supposedly the old Syracusans quipped: 'We're three metres wider than the theatre in Athens!'

I have managed to get a ticket for *The Phoenician Women* by Euripides. Every year, in June and July, a popular festival produces three plays by 'classical' authors: mostly by Euripides, Aeschylus, Aristophanes, sometimes Sophocles as well. At the centre of *The Phoenician Women* is the power struggle between two brothers, both sons of Oedipus, for control of Thebes. At the beginning of the play, Jocasta inducts us into the back story: as foretold by the oracle, Oedipus strikes Laius dead without knowing he is his father, and marries Jocasta without knowing she is his mother. When he discovers his guilt, he blinds himself. The plot is tangled, the dramaturgy complicated, and I quickly lose the thread. In the midst of many thousand attentive spectators, I sit in this immense, steeply raked circle. Two thirds of the *gradini*, the stone seats, are still in the strong evening sun; a third are already in the shade. An ingenious lighting artist achieves a seamless transition from the orange of sunset to cold blue spotlight.

In this bright twilight Teiresias emerges. The blind seer curses the night. The play becomes a wild splatter-story: roaring and murder, curses and blood, evil brother and evil destiny. There is, in effect, no psychology – only *il fato*, fate, simple destiny. Even if I don't understand much, it moves me inwardly. That might have something to do with the theatre's situation, its sheer size, and its significance. I am here at one of the brightest sites of the human spirit. Here on these stone steps, Plato, Aeschylus, Sophocles, Aristippus, and Pindar once sat; there on the *orchestra* stood the imprisoned Athenians; and there he sits, Teiresias, the blinded old man, with his daughter. And the spectators, the Syracusans, look down over their limitless city: on a world once full of temples, colonnaded streets, and magnificent buildings; on two harbours, the small and the great, once named *Marmorena*; and on the sea beyond Plemmirio. You could not imagine a more sublime set design. Still today you may sense something of this old lustre, even though the view over dusty eucalyptus trees to the great harbour has been badly obstructed by new buildings, warehouses, and giant hoardings for supermarkets.

11.

Only the roof terrace of the Hôtel des Étrangers offers a view that is comparable, not for breadth, but for the beauty of the section of the world it presents to you. From here your eyes take in the long-fingered end of the quail island between Porto Grande and the open sea. I have arranged to meet Gaetano Tranchino here for an aperitif. Up here we are entirely transported from the noise, from the tourist swarm around Fonte Aretusa especially. Nothing but silence and golden light on the island city tapering in front of us. Boats glide across the water, noiseless as cats. Three sailboats are lashed together with ropes. Families are celebrating there, have probably already been celebrating the whole summer's day. But they are too far away for us to hear their doubtless wild laughter.

From up here, too, Ortigia is the 'white' city, lapped by a supple sea; nothing like the sombre elegance of the lava city Catania, with its back turned to the water. Nothing is more difficult than capturing a city in words, Gaetano announces, as he sips luxuriantly at his negroni. Everyone who has written about New York has failed. E. L. Doctorow, Paul Auster, Don DeLillo, Harold Brodkey. Syracuse, he continues, which may have been the Manhattan of the Mediterranean 2,500 years ago, has become in the meantime a provincial city.

'So is it easier to portray a city like this one, which isn't tearful but isn't glamorous either?' asks Gaetano.

'I don't know. I'm not sure,' I answer. 'I think Syracuse is a city that is lenient with itself. It doesn't exert itself much. But it's not a complacent city either. I imagine that, whenever it wants to feel sorry for itself, it inwardly calls itself to order. Whatever happens, it does not want to be overwhelmed by its own memories, still less be slain by them.'

'Perhaps it's not an advantage to have a great past,' muses Gaetano. 'But the Syracusans face up to their past and, in their own way, in some hidden way, they are proud of it.'

12.

That evening, back home, I read Ferdinand Gregorovius's *Wanderings in Italy* on the darkening terrace. When he was in Syracuse in 1855 and looked down from the high plateau onto the area of the old city, he compared it to a wasteland. 'As far as the eye can see,' he noted, 'she has been ransacked and gouged by the grave-stinking centuries and by the tracks of countless ages. She is like one vast battlefield of history.' At another point, he speaks of the 'the endless killing fields of Syracuse'.

Gregorovius had come here at a time when the city was in a state of extreme paralysis. Like the rest of Sicily, Syracuse had fallen under the rule of the House of Bourbon-Two Sicilies, an Italian cadet branch of the Spanish Bourbons. Since 1817, the capital of the 'King of Two Sicilies' had been Naples. Sicily sank into lethargy, bled dry by rapacious Spanish administrators, who instituted a police state. Here is Gregorovius again: 'Today the modern race of Syracusans meander along the quay of the great harbour, joyless, feeble, without scholarship, without art, without industry; they are sunk like villagers into the most narrow and restricted life and reduced to slavery under the loathed Naples.'

Better times did not arrive until the *Risorgimento*, the struggle for an independent Italian nation state, the arrival of Garibaldi at Marsala in May 1860, and the defeat of the Bourbon forces. Italian unification changed Syracuse as well. Freed from stifling police surveillance, the city began to modernise itself. The Spanish fortifications were razed. The huge city gates, decorated with a hideous opulence and known to me only from old photogravures, were blown up. For the first time in centuries the city expanded back onto the 'mainland', building on the derelict old Greek districts of the city: Achradina, Tyche, and especially Neapolis, that 'new city' where the Greek Theatre, the Roman amphitheatre, and the *latomie* are situated. An elegant quarter of villas and town houses in a uniform classical style rose up around Corso Umberto. Trade increased. A railway connected Syracuse to Messina and Catania. The city grew rapidly, especially eastwards along the coast as far as the Capuchin monastery. Several since dilapidated but still splendid Art Nouveau villas, not least Villa Politi, stand witness to this moment to this day.

13.

Coming from Ortigia, cross over the bridge into the new town and you will be struck by the upper-class houses that line Corso Umberto and the neighbouring streets. Then turn right towards the small marina on Viale Regina Margherita, which merges into Via dell'Arsenale, and you will notice a row of opulent villas, in a dark-red wash, overgrown with ancient stands of trees, huge yuccas, and candelabra cactuses, and deluged by cascades of dark-red bougainvillea. All of these town houses and villas were built, I would estimate, either before or shortly after the turn of the century, in classical style with touches of Art Nouveau and, in the later buildings, early Art Deco influences.

You find villas of the same type all around the Mediterranean, in Sorrento, Naples, Marseille, Beirut, and Alexandria, where Italian architects designed the grandest villas. Here in Neapolis these houses allow us to imagine how beautiful and inviting Syracuse must have been at the turn of the century – and on until the late 1930s. The building of eyesores began in the 1950s and continued for more than twenty years. Concrete hulks sprang up everywhere. A corrupt bureaucracy authorised 'modernisation'. Profiteering and selfishness defeated the plans of the archaeologist Luigi Bernabò Brea, who had drafted a visionary plan immediately after the Second World War to turn Neapolis into a single archaeological zone, with large parks, more museums, and limited development, subject to strict conditions. All of which came to nothing. Tall apartment blocks encircled the old two-storey houses. Only a few escaped demolition.

These left-over architectural delights include Villa Landolina, now in the gardens of the Paolo Orsi Archaeological Museum, Villa Politi, and Villa Reimann, which is located behind the Archaeological Park, on Via Necropoli Grotticelli. This street name – I translate it boldly and badly as 'Little Grotto Graves Street' – is more than appropriate, as the gardens of the villa contain offshoots of the Latomia and walkers there will come across overgrown caves. The villa itself was erected in 1881–2, commissioned by the Senator Cocuzza in honour of the then very famous Spanish singer Fegotto. Her name still graces the medallion over the entrance portal. Christiane Reimann, a Danish woman born in 1888 who studied in New York, was a devotee of Florence Nightingale, and worked for the International Council of Nurses in Geneva, came to Syracuse for the first time in 1935. She fell in love with the city and purchased Villa Fegotto in the same year. Reimann, known in Syracuse as 'our Karen Blixen', was a passionate gardener. She introduced rare and exotic plants and turned the grounds of the villa into an oasis of garden artistry, sociability and peace.

It was not until the war years that this idyll was disturbed. Because Reimann maintained links with the International Red Cross, the villa became a point of contact for everyone seeking missing persons and prisoners. The local authorities viewed these activities with suspicion and forced Reimann to abandon the villa and move her place of residence to Floridia. But this was not the end of her troubles. After they had occupied Sicily and taken Syracuse, the Allies installed their headquarters in Villa Reimann, allocating just one room to its owner.

It would be several years before the villa became again what it had been before the war: a magnificent building in well-laid-out gardens with a view over the stone quarries and the old necropolis and on to the distant sea.

14.

I had things to do in Berlin. When I got back to Ortigia two weeks later and climbed up the steps onto my terrace, to assure myself that the Ionian Sea had been waiting for me with stoic calm, it occurred to me that things were unusually quiet down on Piazza del Precursore. I sifted my post, fetched my book (the Gregorovius), uncorked a bottle of wine, and began to read. Only after some time did I realise what was missing: Ronny's yapping. Evidently Ronny was not there. I bent over the balustrade and looked down. The door on the little balcony opposite was shut, the blinds were fully lowered, even the window next to the door had wooden shutters bolted across it. That was unusual. Monteleone didn't travel anymore. There was no way he could. Had he fallen ill? Was he lying in hospital? I suddenly felt a great emptiness inside me and in the same instant was so unsettled that I walked to the little café on the corner of Via della Giudecca. The owner, who played the monotonous piano pieces of Einaudi day and night, told me that Monteleone was dead.

Sure, he had been ill, we all knew that, no longer the youngest, his legs, his hips, his breathing difficulties. But then he'd had a gastric haemorrhage in the night. An aorta had burst. He couldn't make it to the phone. The ambulance didn't come until morning. Much too late.

'And was there a funeral service, a burial?' I asked.

'Already happened last week. His son came from Milan and settled everything. He doesn't want to keep the apartment. He's instructed an agent to sell it.'

I was dumbfounded. Just now Giuseppe Monteleone was still here and in the next moment, no longer. I remembered that he had shown me his apartment in the last year. It was huge – with four rooms, a large kitchen, two bathrooms, one with shower, the other with an expansive bathtub. But his age and his trouble with his hips had forced him to shrink his life into one room, the room with the narrow balcony that looked out onto the piazza. In this room he had rigged up two keyboards and there were drums lying around on the floor, a guitar, an accordion. Next to the table was a wingback chair in yellow upholstery, which he slept in at night as well, a huge TV and a cupboard next to it, which he opened for me. My eyes fell on perhaps eight dozen cans of food.

'Everything I need to eat is here,' he had said cheerily. 'Tinned tomatoes, pasta, *vongole*, *salame morbido* and so on.'

Shortly before I departed for Berlin we had had dinner again at Bianco Pepe. I had invited him and Dora and Alberto too and he had managed the short distance from his front door to the table set up directly outside on the square pretty well, with the aid of a stick. We talked about his music room and how ravishingly he still played. He told us about his parents, who had had a great respect for education. His family lived in a suburb of Catania. His first instrument had been an accordion. He played for the neighbours in the day and in the air-raid shelter at night. This was 1943 and he was seven years old. It would have been possible to combine the two things, no problem, he said, playing music and becoming a policeman. But he didn't join the police band. He was into other things, light music, circus music even, not military marches.

At that dinner, which I could have had no inkling would be our last with him, I wanted to hear from him what his most thrilling 'cases' had been as a detective in Syracuse. Dora backed me up: 'Just tell us, Giuseppe! Don't make a fuss! Come on!'

He stroked his white side-whiskers, raised his glass of wine, and smiled all around him. 'Well, okay. My years as a detective. That was probably the most exciting time for me. Most of it was drug-related. Two Tunisians were smuggling dope in boats from Morocco to Cap Bon and from there to here, Syracuse and Pachino. The Mafia had their fingers in the pie as well. They were running one of the Tunisians. It was difficult to get those two. The whole thing was not undangerous.'

But he didn't want to cough up any details. He acted as if he were still on duty and had to preserve his professional secrets.

I tried another way. 'Are there many drug addicts in Syracuse?' I wanted to know.

'We mustn't criminalise them,' he said. 'Otherwise, in the end, there are only losers. The consumers didn't really interest me. It was more the dealers.'

Giuseppe was astonishingly full of life that evening. He indulged in the *rosso* and, all his frailties notwithstanding, put on the charm, praising Dora's trembling earrings and announcing that – had it not already been evening – he would have happily taken a siesta in her blonde hair.

'Of course,' was Alberto's response, as if Giuseppe wasn't misbehaving.

Ronny stayed up on the small balcony throughout our meal, looking down at us. He howled once. That was when Clara's elastic cats showed themselves on the Juliet balcony next door.

Now I'm wondering what has become of Ronny. He was entirely fixated on his master, paranoid, a neurotic, a psychopath. I doubt he could live without Monteleone, or would want to. He's probably been taken by force to an animal shelter. He will be there now, riled and aggressive, because that is just how he is, barking at the other inmates and biting until he is bitten. A tragedy.

15.

On Via Nizza I have many times walked heedlessly past a shop, which I never even recognised as a shop; what people called in Germany a hundred years ago a 'colonial goods store'. It does, to be fair, make itself hard to recognise. Its two windows are just windows, pretty filthy and with nothing on display. Its door is mostly closed and off-putting. In summer, multi-coloured strings of beads hang down in the doorway in some nondescript pattern. But trespass across that threshold and a dusty paradise unveils itself before you. From the ceiling hangs what you might describe, with some imagination, as a knock-off of a shabby Venetian chandelier. On one side jute sacks are stored cheek by jowl with their 'snouts' open, filled with potatoes, broad beans, purple onions, carob, and dried goods I cannot identify. On the opposite side, three dozen long, hefty nails have been bashed into the wall. From them hang garlands of onions, plaits of garlic, dried peppers, and sausages, which look like they were formed by the fat hands of a butcher decades ago. Facing the entrance is a long vitrine. On tiered shelves behind the lightly fogged glass there is pretty much everything that milk can bring forth, from yoghurt to mozzarella, and some very rustic-looking wheels of cheese. For slightly more refined products, however, I seek in vain. Next to the vitrine stands a white-painted counter with a large, old set of scales enthroned upon it. The weight pointer trembles in the middle of a triangle stood on its point, next to a metal bowl, where the goods are placed for weighing.

After I had discovered this shop, I wished that the old couple that ran it would set a small table with two wobbly chairs in the middle of the space. I would go there late in the morning, order two fat slices of mortadella and a bowl of pistachios and to go with them, a glass of Muscat, which makes my spirits leap. Unfortunately Rosaria and Ignazio have not understood even my cruder signals. Perhaps they also simply do not want to change anything or are no longer in a position to do so.

16.

A hundred times I've travelled in a bus or taxi on the exit road towards Avola and the motorway to Catania past the high, yellow-brown wall of the *cimitero*, the municipal cemetery. This time I resolve to pay a visit. The way in is amicably lined with flower stalls, the only ones in the city. Step through the wide iron gates and you arrive immediately into a close-packed city of the dead. Every clan has its own mausoleum, house of the dead next to house of the dead, and there are, as I soon discover, actual high-rises of the dead, with two, three, four storeys, connected by staircases, where the deceased rest in their hundreds. Some of these large houses were built by religious orders but most were built by congregations, each with a particular orientation.

The alleyways edged by these stone mausoleums alternate with withered, yellow fallow fields dotted with modest graves. The nineteenth-century bourgeoisie had veritable houses built for their dead to live on in, while the workers, the fishermen, lie in tiny patches of these fields, if they are not accommodated in the thousands upon thousands of niches for urns. These 'burial walls' look from a distance like endless, vertically arranged coffered ceilings, each coffer with a concrete closure, desiccated flowers, and a photo of the person who has died. These people grew astonishingly old, even those born before 1900, often to eighty, eighty-five, or ninety years old.

To the left of the temple of rest, a rotunda which from a distance looks like a mini-Pantheon, is the section that shakes me most. Here lie the young dead, the stillborn, the newborn. On the plaques I read 'NM' with a single year.

Does that mean *nato* and *morto* in the same year or *nato morto*, born dead? The little graves are conspicuously decorated, much more colourful than all the others. On many of the stones are the words '*Mama Papi ti amo*' and a small, blonde angel's head, captured in an already bleached-out colour photograph, looking down at their favourite toys: Lego bricks, unicorns, Barbies.

Strange though it may sound, a walk around the cemetery has often been for me, alongside my visit to the hairdresser's, a proven means to unlock a city. In the cemeteries of Genoa, Trieste, Budapest, Paris, you learn a great deal about the melancholic veins of those cities. I hoped for something similar from the *cimitero* in Syracuse. The houses of the dead, built in Art Deco style, remind me particularly of the tops of the pyramids in Uxmal or Palenque, Mayan temples in the Mexican jungle, tropically washed out, yellowish, greenish, mighty. Here in Syracuse there is no jungle, but there are giant, ancient, knotted cypresses, archaic palms, and stone-old, broad-spread ficus trees with their enormous aerial roots. And there is an unending silence, total stillness. No cicadas. No birds, except – once – the distant cooing of a dove. No lizards. Only the soughing of palm fronds. Only the crackling of dried flowers. Only the shuffling of cleaning women, who keep the grand families' houses of the dead free from spiders and gecko droppings. I did not find the grave of Giuseppe Monteleone. Everything dismal. Everything ringed by an unending desolation. On the horizon, karst.

17.

How much lovelier, almost idyllic by comparison, is the final resting place of August, Count von Platen, which I tracked down on the edge of the gardens of Count Landolina. We must in fact speak of resting places, given that the Franconian poet was laid to rest three times: immediately after his death, then again in 1869, and lastly, one further time, on the centenary of his demise. That was 1935 and the memorial service was tinged with pompous nationalism, if not downright fascism, for which the poor poet can take no blame. Platen's continued resonance in Sicily must be related to his early death in Syracuse and his burial there. A delegation from Bavaria and his home town of Ansbach travelled to attend the solemn erection of the stele in 1869. The Bavarian minister-president, Prince Chlodwig of Hohenlohe, sent a fervid telegram of mourning. The geologist and Etna researcher Baron Wolfgang Sartorius von Waltershausen led the travelling committee. The eulogies were numerous and classes of girls from Syracuse's elementary schools laid posies and laurel wreaths at the foot of the stele.

Neither at this ceremony, nor during the solemnities of 1935, nor in the volumes of poetry published in Italian translation to mark both occasions, was there any mention of August von Platen's two Sicilian poems, 'Hymn from Sicily' and 'In Palermo'. In his 'Hymn', Platen holds the kidnapping of Persephone and her carrying off into the underworld to be determining events in Sicily's fate: 'And since this country shed / her lovely care, it languishes in indolent, immeasurable, enchanted sleep ...'. Evidently this 'indolent

... enchanted sleep' of the Sicilians didn't go down well with those organising these events – nor indeed the following passage on how Sicily was conquered by the 'heroes of Germania'.

Re-reading Tomasi di Lampedusa's *The Leopard*, I found a startling correspondence with Platen's vision of the Sicilian 'enchanted sleep'. In the famous dialogue between the prince and the Piedmontese envoy Aimone Chevalley, Tomasi has the prince voice this quintessentially Platenish sentiment: 'Sleep, my dear Chevalley, sleep, that is what the Sicilians want, and they will always hate anyone who tries to wake them, even in order to bring them the most wonderful of gifts.'

18.

Back at the market today. The giant eyes of the swordfish greet me. Apart from the eyes and the heads that belong with them, everything has already been hacked away, sliced up, sold off, wolfed down. Next to them are the blood-red blocks of tuna and the silvery white of the *spigola*. In the past I used to walk to the market every day, even if I had nothing to buy, for the sheer joy of all the colours, shapes, and smells in the pale pink light under the awnings. The market is Ortigia's noisily seething belly.

But like everything in Ortigia, the market street has changed over the years. With the exception of Borderi, famous for its *panini* with sky-high fillings, and of Fratelli Burgio, the superior delicatessen, in the past there were only stalls for fruit, vegetables, spices, and fish. Also stalls for nuts, dried fruit, various olive oils, and speciality cheeses. Now the spice shop has metamorphosed into a takeaway and other pitches are increasingly being used to run diners and hot-food stalls. Like markets in Berlin, Madrid, or Paris, my beloved market is mutating more and more into a feeding street. There are reasons why. People are less and less willing to spend their time cooking. A good meal made from fresh ingredients can take two or three hours to prepare: studying the recipe, going shopping, dicing and slicing, and stewing and roasting. Explanation enough for fast food's victory parade. It conjures an image of a human race that only ever gulps down ready meals and little by little devours the world. The children here, who always seemed so lithe and slim and alert, are growing fatter. My image of Italy is tottering.

After several rain-soaked weeks, the antiquarian bookseller has finally set out his stall on the market again, encircled by mountains of artichokes and pyramids of oranges. I find a book I've been seeking for a long time, a compilation of tourist advertising posters for Syracuse from 1950 to 2003. In retrospect these posters look uniformly staid, stale even. The graphic designers who produced them may have been exciting forty or fifty years ago, but that doesn't come across any more, and their visual vocabulary is starkly limited: papyrus sedge, the Landolina Venus, the amphitheatre, the cathedral façade. Sun. Really not much else.

Looking at the posters for events, I'm struck by how much more was going on in Syracuse thirty years ago: Argentinian dance groups, the Martha Graham Dance

Company, the Bolshoi at the Greek Theatre in 1992. In September 1997 the award ceremony for the Premio Vittorini, with Manuel Vázquez Montalbán and Giulio Einaudi, took place in the Great Hall, followed by a *Carosello Equestre* by the *carabinieri*. Imagine it: the prize-giving shrouded in clouds of sawdust and shot through with pyrotechnic highlights. Why doesn't something like that happen today? Why is the Teatro Comunale so very dead?

'What do the people of Catania make of this dead Syracuse?' I ask Dora Suma. I've bumped into her at the market and am sipping a *caffè* with her at Burgio.

'Catania is Marrakesh!' exclaims Dora. 'The Catanese are traders. They're in it for the buying and selling and they want to make a profit. They envy Syracuse.'

'How so?'

'To them, the Syracusans are Greeks. Serious Greeks. Greeks who don't have much of a clue about wheeling and dealing.' After a pause she adds: 'The Syracusans like to look at the sea, at the ships. They are, if you like, inclined to contemplate. You could also say, they are slow on the uptake.'

Fundamentally, Dora is right. Unless you're in the middle of some alleyway overstuffed with tourists, Ortigia moves at a rather settled pace, and at siesta time on Piazza del Precursore an otherworldly, almost unsettling quiet descends.

19.

Things are livelier in the summer months on the solariums. By *solarium*, the Sicilians mean a large platform made of fixed, joined-together sheets of chipboard on an iron framework over the sea. On most, steps lead directly from this 'sun terrace' into the water. Just under two hundred metres from my apartment, down narrow Via Minniti, you arrive at the Spanish bastion Vigliena. There, on the rocky shore, a solarium stands, built by the Commune at the beginning of summer, generally in mid-June, and then dismantled again in mid-October before the autumn storms. In the hot months I swim there often two or three times a day, sometimes the first time before breakfast. The water then is superb, washed clean by the night, caressing and boundlessly clear.

Come here regularly to swim as I do and you begin to notice the different visitors at each time of day. Very early, the 'sporty types' assemble: sinewy men, women too, with flippers, sometimes for hands as well as feet, and sleek bathing caps that match their resolute features. Mostly they swim crawl from the bastion to Castello Maniace and back – about four kilometres.

Between nine and ten the older ladies make their entrance. Decked out with green earrings and glass bead necklaces, they seat themselves next to the solarium on one of the many rocks at the water's edge and let the water lap up to the knee on their old, knotted, parchment-skin legs. Most of the time they are in small groups of two or three women who know each other and chatter without pause as the water murmurs. The colour of their skin reminds me of farmers in the far south of India. One morning, when I arrived to swim, about twenty pairs of flip-flops were garnishing the top of the steps leading down to the water. Unbidden, the thought came to me of a mosque where the faithful remove their shoes. Here a school form had climbed down into the water along with their teacher, who had transplanted their lesson into the watery element.

From eleven, a rather motley crew approaches: tourists, older couples from the neighbourhood, and a few young people, who have just left their beds and had their *colazione*. The really trendy among the young people avoid the solarium and walk onto the large, broad rock connected by a footbridge to the main rock, where the bastion stands. From there it is a superb three-metre plunge into the deep Ionian Sea. On this rock, as much as on the solarium, there is constant, lively change. Later, single women come, evidently from the poorer classes. They remind me of the lonely women in Cesare Pavese, the dressmakers and shop assistants of Turin.

From 5 p.m., the fans of the late colours appear. The sea is beautifully weary and a fraction warmer than in the morning. A handful of veterans mingle with the neighbourhood's youth. One of them, with a luxuriant snow-white wreath of hair, comes always with his dog. This dog is an impressive swimmer, following his master far out into the open sea. One pot-bellied man from Via Veneto, where he runs an antiques shop, sometimes brings a fat, reddish cat under his arm. The cat swims with him, indeed is visibly delighted to do so. It is the only cat in the world, that I know of, that does this. Still later, four *ragazzi* arrive sporting fantastical tattoos on their thighs and lower legs. They have taken it into their heads to conquer the solarium at sunset and turn it into a football pitch. They are successful. The final bathers melt away in the face of these dazzling nerds. They let the ball roll from lower leg to heel to instep until, by some magic trick, it lands back on the head and from there rolls away onto the back heel of the neighbouring player. At one point the ball falls into the water and one of the four, a sinewy red-haired guy, jumps in, stumbles over the smooth stones, abruptly yelps: '*Una medusa!*' and shows us his red wrist, instantly angrily swollen from contact with the jellyfish stingers.

20.

For more than seven years, night after night, I have watched the recurring light of the lighthouse that stands at the tip of Plemmirio, guiding ships into Porto Grande. Its counterpart, the lighthouse on the Ortigia side, is mounted onto a corner of Castello Maniace, stout and painted green.

Today is the day. I rent a Fiat 500 Plus at 'Sicily by Car' on Corso Umberto. I want, finally, to visit the lighthouse on Plemmirio and explore the peninsula at the same time. The lighthouse has a curious name: *Faro di Capo Murro di Porco*. Some think this is a reference to the rocky extremity of the cape, which resembles a pig's snout.

Everything on Plemmirio is hard to find. The tangle of small roads and tracks is large and the absence of street signs total. Several times I arrive at the sea via a cul-de-sac that peters out in the rocky nowhere. The closer I come to the tip of the peninsula, the sparser the vegetation, the stonier the ground. Eventually there is only gravel, thorny weeds, a few fan palms. Here the great ashlars for the temples of Minerva and Apollo were cut from the rock formations on the coast and carried by ship – evidently this was easier than by land – to Ortigia.

At last I reach the cape on which the lighthouse stands. A low building sits in front of the octagonal, whitewashed tower, on the landward side. Presumably this houses the keeper's accommodation and machine rooms with all the technical supplies. It is a purely functional building, the original symmetry of the windows disturbed by alterations, the plaster crumbling. In the winter the weather must be hellish: scourging winds, tremendous gusts, immense breakers with surf as high as a house. Unfortunately access to the building is forbidden, but there isn't very much more to see anyway. A feeling of contentment comes over me. Now I know exactly where the white light is coming from, which casts its beam across the Ionian Sea to Ortigia at intervals of fifteen seconds. From a very lonely tower. From a cheerless place. From a horizon empty of humans in every direction. As I make my way home, I think how in 3,000 years nothing has changed on this cape of Plemmirio. An image of pure inhospitality.

21.

Every Sunday the otherwise metaphysically quiet Piazza Santa Lucia in the Borgata district is transformed into a clamouring flea market. Quantities of junk are spread out on shaky tables: old vinyl records, toys, knock-off ceramics, fruits made of coloured glass, nineteenth-century prints nibbled by silverfish showing interiors from a hedonistic, orientalist Greece. Any amount of tattered books. More than all the goods on display it is the customers that intrigue me: the *flâneurs*, especially the women, who on this warm day are showing off their splendour on astonishingly short legs.

As I look at them, I am reminded of the peculiar chapter on Syracuse in George Russell's *A Tour through Sicily in the Year 1815*, in which he bundles together papyrus plants, the mouth of the Ciane River, climate, grapevines, and women in an astonishing fashion. On the women, he doesn't have much to say:

> The women of *Syracuse* are, generally speaking, well made, and retain, even at the present day, much of that *Grecian* contour of countenance for which they were formerly so justly praised. They dress in a very becoming and truly chaste style, and still wear their veil in the same elegant manner as the celebrated Queen *Philistides* of antiquity is represented on the different medallions. Many of the young females of this city are as beautiful and lovely in person as they are lively and agreeable in conversation; they are besides extremely fascinating in their general manners, accomplished, and sound their favourite instrument the guitar in a very superior way, accompanying themselves at the same time with sweet melodious sonnets.

Russell appears not to recognise originality. He continues even more woodenly:

> The greater part of the females of *Sicily* marry ... extremely young, that is, between fourteen and seventeen years of age, and consequently become as it were old at a very early period of life. *Theocritus* ... has very correctly described in his twenty-third *Idyllium* this

apparent early decay of beauty .... In a word, the peculiar softness of the climate, the delicious flavour of the wines, and the irresistible fascination of lovely woman, all united, inspire the highest pleasure and delight.

Could anyone top that? Russell himself proves it is possible. As his travelling party is leaving the city for Catania and Etna and their muleteer announces at a bend in the road that this could be the last time they will be able to see Syracuse, the travellers spontaneously cry out: 'Adieu, oh! metamorphosed, yet splendid *Syracusa*! – Adieu, oh! greatly fallen, yet magnificent *Syracusa*! – Adieu, charming *Syracusa*! – Once more, we bid thee adieu!'

22.

I am making more excursions. You might think that Ortigia has begun to bore me. But I'm only heeding the call of friends, who have settled down in the area around Noto and Syracuse and want to be visited.

Today I took the Interbus to Pachino to meet Elena Montagna, who, along with her husband, the actor Enrico Lo Verso, had just bought a farmstead in dire need of restoration on the edge of Vendicari. Our meeting point was Caffè al Ciclope on the central square of this small town. 'Piazza Vittorio Emanuele has its territories,' Elena told me. 'The right-hand corner with the benches belongs to the retired fishermen. This corner is the old farmers' and the other corner over there is for the unemployed and those of independent means.'

On my journey here from Syracuse I noticed several

beautiful squares that I had missed on an earlier trip along the south coast. In Avola three huge black lions crouched around a fountain, as if around a glittering watering hole. Another of Avola's squares was entirely surrounded by blossoming jacaranda trees, which had no leaves yet. It was like blue confetti, like a giant azure cloud, hovering over the fountain.

After an especially delicious *granite ai mirtilli*, a speciality of the Cyclops, we headed on to Portopalo, Sicily's southernmost point. A sandy bay of green, endlessly clear water invited us to swim. Enrico was waiting for us in a simple local restaurant on the harbour above some rotten fishing boats. He had ordered us a magnificent meal. Raw, reddish prawns, elegant, orange-coloured shrimps and tiny breaded octopuses were heaped into a sculpture it was our joy to ruin. *Benissimo!*

Enrico turned the conversation to Pier Paolo Pasolini, who wrote a travel piece in 1959 for *Successo*, a big celebrity lifestyle magazine of its day, which had led him to Portopalo too. The title: *La Lunga Strada di Sabbia – The Long Road of Sand*. Pasolini drove along the entire Italian coast in a little Fiat: from Ventimiglia and Sanremo down the Tyrrhenian coast via Ostia and Amalfi as far as Messina; then along the Ionian coast via Catania and Syracuse; and finally back up the entire Adriatic coast, from Brindisi and Bari via Pescara and Riccione to Trieste. Time and again he describes moments of complete happiness, intoxicated by colours, by smells, by a 'moon bigger than I've ever seen before'. Enrico spoke of Pasolini's ability to be happy in spite of his despair, in spite of his acute experience of transience. The same qualities that make his poems so strong, so resilient.

Back home, I search out the book and re-read the entire passage. Pasolini arrives in Syracuse in July 1959. At the Hôtel des Étrangers he comes across a poster advertising a performance of Shakespeare's *The Winter's Tale* in one of the *latomie* and listing the cast, or at least the well-known ones. He discovers the name of Adriana Asti, an actress he reveres and is friends with. He looks for her and eventually finds her at Villa Politi. 'We embrace, shouting,' he writes, 'get into the car, and we're off, to the sea of Siracusa. "You know, it's fantastic here! I'm never going to leave," Adriana exclaims to me, "I'll have myself abducted by a Sicilian Baron – there were dozens of them circling around me in Palermo!"'

The prose of Pasolini's reportage is simple but with a beautiful, catchy rhythm. I don't believe the magazine imposed this style on him. He is speaking about his happiness and so searches for a new simplicity of language to do so. Here is a longer passage, to illustrate my point:

As if we'd planned it, the Anapo river runs along our road. We're hardly going to pass up this opportunity. We turn inland onto a dusty little road, along an intensely aromatic field of liquorice, and there, bordered by a line of olive trees, carobs, and prickly pears, is the Anapo, splashing away green and warm, its current full of papyrus. 'Papyrus, papyrus!' Adriana shouts happily.

'They only exist here and in Egypt, did you know that?'
A young guy who is passing by hears her and – no, I'm
not exaggerating – he has an ancient face, truly, I can't
really tell whether it's Phoenician, Alexandrian, or of
some Roman-southern Italian scribe, and one of those
backs with the protuberant shoulders that you only see
on painted vases. This youth, saying nothing, runs down
the bright green bank of the Anapo and pulls up three
long reeds of papyrus with their slender green fringe at
the top. He gives them to Adriana, who takes them full
of happiness and clutches them in her hand.

This section of the book ends in Portopalo, the village
where I feasted today at lunch with Elena and Enrico,
exactly at the point where the Ionian Sea meets the African
Mediterranean, looking out at a tiny island dominated by
a fortification from the time of the Spanish. Pasolini has a
young man row him there across a small stretch of water,
and as night encroaches, bathes 'at the poorest and remot-
est beach in Italy.'

23.
'You're an enemy of the spirit level?'

'How do you come up with that?' asks Gaetano, who I
am visiting again in his studio after a long gap. I've been
there a while already.

'Very simple. There are no straight lines in your pictures. Everything undulates. As if a gentle wind is blowing
through the forms, a gondola rising on every wave.'

'What you call "undulation", that comes from Etna.

Everything quakes a little. It keeps on erupting, as you know. Volcanoes are like that. That causes tectonic shifts, which you can still feel in Syracuse.'

'And that causes lopsided balconies, butchered fan palms, and broken columns?'

'I have to confess something terrible to you. I'm tired of my vocabulary. This whole arsenal of forms and symbols. This island is enchanting, but somehow paralysing as well. Why did all the important artists leave Sicily? Guttuso, Pirandello, Vittorini. They went to Rome, to Milan. Some of them came back to their island, strengthened by other things, replenished. Others, like Vittorini, stayed away. I should have had the strength to leave at some point. But I've always stayed on Ortigia. Now I've tried something new. I'll show you a few of the new things, if you have time.'

From the rear of his studio, he brings forward one canvas after another and places them on one of the three easels in the front of the room, where the light is so much better. They are peculiar pictures. Roads in a southern landscape. White lines on asphalt. A dressmaker's pattern, markings. Directions to turn, to stop. I see a car bonnet, a stretch of road, the beginning of a curve. Some of the images are of evening, with headlights cutting trees out of the darkness, also undergrowth by the side of the road, which is aflame, beautiful to look at.

'These are my exploratory moves,' says Gaetano. 'Perhaps it's all bullshit. But they've kept me very busy for a few weeks.'

The pictures are odd. They don't excite me and he can feel it.

'Exploratory moves?' I ask. 'Leading where?'

'Oh, come on! You understand that better than I do. Your poetry, that's exploratory too. Resisting the loss of your powers of poetic expression.'

24.

Could today's Syracuse lead a philosopher into temptation, just as Plato was tempted, long, long ago, by a city of the same name? On my walks around Ortigia and the new town, I pose myself this question over and over. There was, I believe, no word in Ancient Greek to correspond to *Mezzogiorno*, the term that was first applied in the nineteenth century to the south of Italy, the poor region, and to Sicily, the southernmost extremity, the poorest region, which was hot in summer, parched and fissured, plagued by earthquakes and other catastrophes. At the time of *Magna Graecia*, which was Plato's time as well, Sicily was considered a thriving island, rich in cereals and vegetables, a larder for the rest of the Greek world. And in the midst of this garden nestled Syracuse, the lustrous capital.

None of that could be said now and every other attraction that could have drawn Plato and his like is missing too. There are no more tyrants displaying philosophical or artistic leanings. The ruling class is entirely unimaginative. The ruler of Syracuse is a dull local politician, a party tactician without the means to inspire, or even strike a spark. The four-time mayor of Palermo, Leoluca Orlando, is perhaps the only one who possessed enough charisma to have, for a few years, put artists and intellectuals under his spell.

Cities rarely think about their declines. Most happen not suddenly, by war or disaster, but slowly and in torturous stages. Or a mix of the two. The great earthquake of 1693 was such a disaster. But Syracuse did not move to another location to resurrect itself, as Noto and Avola did. Ortigia could not be abandoned; its people remained within the confines of the island. The Baroque rebuilding had a predetermined shape. That's one reason for the beautiful uniformity of the old quarter, with its balconies, its ornamentation, its windows and doors edged with honey-white sandstone.

It was a gentle fall, over the centuries. From the million-strong metropolis of the fourth century BC to the provincial city of around 120,000 inhabitants at the end of the nineteenth century, one contraction followed another, dwindling and dwindling, sinking. The Romans were plunderers who looted Syracuse; the Byzantines, and after them the Arabs, brought no upturn; the Normans concerned themselves almost exclusively with Palermo; the Spanish thought only strategically and militarily. All no good for the city. Had Syracuse had a special function – gateway to North Africa, most important port on the way to Alexandria and the Levant – its journey into retirement would likely have been even more difficult. The inspiration that once brought Syracuse fame and respect, a compound of beautiful landscape and magnificent cultural inheritance, is gone. Today the inspiration is money, the ideology, materialism. That sounds harsh. And yet because the old greatness still shines through, because it must not be forgotten, this special power persists and, as we make our circuit of Ortigia, we sense it.

I sense this power in conversations with my friends here as well. They draw it from their island's place on the periphery and, it is hard to believe, from a melancholy that grows from their not-forgetting of its history.

25.

Keyword: melancholy. What have I been doing all this time? The days go by, you sleep, you wake up, you fall in love afresh with the sight of the Ionian Sea, you doze with half-closed eyes in the midday sun, indolent as a gecko, you swim, you seek the shade, you make a few notes, these notes, and you ask yourself whether they will endure.

Now, because in a short while I am flying to Berlin and must say my goodbyes to Syracuse for a couple of weeks, my thoughts are circling, as so often, around this city. In comparison with the Syracuse that Seume saw, that Gregorovius still experienced as an 'antiquarian desert', which was perhaps still present in a much weakened form in the 1950s when Vincenzo Consolo came to the city, I sense in today's Ortigia a general movement towards the present tense of life, in which the remains of Greek and Roman times may once again reveal their friendly power. The deeper layers are still there, even where they are wholly overgrown. In his book on Sicily, the famous German sociologist René König speaks very beautifully of 'a seamless unity of life'.

Ortigia's cathedral represents this unity. There are structures that symbolise a city and its history, where you may grasp the memory of the past in the physical substance of today, where contemplation and remembrance are in dialogue with the layers of stone. The cathedral holds this dialogue. The new element, the baroque, is so visible in the outer layer of the building that you might expect it to end up a fiasco. But here it convinces. The feeling almost throughout is of calm inevitability, as if the temple-cathedral had been completed in its sleep, in that measureless sleep of which Tomasi di Lampedusa speaks.

26.

Lucio calls me and says that that his 'colleague' Baron Pietro Beneventano del Bosco has invited him to a private concert at his palace tomorrow. Even if I don't feel like it, I should come along. I do feel like it. The Beneventanos own the largest palace on the cathedral square. Bourbon kings, Admiral Nelson, Lady Hamilton, his Emma, and other celebrated men and their mistresses of fabled beauty have spent the night there. Beneventano himself is considered a significant collector of autograph manuscripts and documents on the city's history, as well as a gifted storyteller. All of this makes me extremely curious. On top of which, I am keen to meet another example of the Sicilian nobility.

Recently I met Paola, who runs the Hotel Gutkowski. She told me about her mother, who, like her grandmother, the famous *marquesa*, loved extravagances and held court at her estate in Cassibile. 'Once again I had to conclude when

I visited that there wasn't much going on in my mother's head. It drove me to despair.' And she added: 'You know that the aristocrats here in Sicily have their latifundia. They have or had a lot of money. They drifted, floundering and thoughtless, from party to party, from Grand Hotel to Grand Hotel, from gaming hall to casino. My grandmother included. She was tall and slim, with that smooth stride that the Venetians called the 'greyhound-bitch's walk'. I wouldn't like to know how many affairs she had before she met this Gutkowski, this handsome Polish officer, and gave all her other suitors the elbow.'

This conversation comes back into my head on my way to Palazzo Beneventano. The palace in all its baroque finery presents itself to the eye as the culmination of Piazza Minerva. I walk along the Doric columns that emerge from the wall of the cathedral and tell myself, as I have so often before, that this is a city of conflicting destinies, between glory and oblivion. The Arabs in Syracuse have been completely forgotten. The hated Spanish are still present only because they had all of Ortigia rebuilt in their own style after the great earthquake. And the Hohenstaufen Frederick II, though he was hardly ever here, is revered as a demigod. Archimedes, perhaps the most significant Syracusan, the genius of Greek Sicily, remains a legend, between imagination and reality. And with these thoughts, I step into the vast inner courtyard of the Palazzo.

Lucio has announced my arrival. Our hosts, Barone Pietro and Baronessa Rosanna, are standing on the top landing of the outdoor staircase and welcome me warmly. They lead me through an enfilade of rooms, past a gigantic green billiard table and a plethora of console tables, credenzas, and dark ancestral portraits, covering the walls in tight clusters, and on into a large, rectangular, and airy salon, in which it is the painted ceiling, because it is so lightly and playfully achieved, that fascinates me most of all. The five tall French windows look out directly onto the façade of the cathedral and the town hall devised by the architect Vermexio. The concert is to take place in this room.

There is not much time for conversation or to get to know each other. The players in the quartet from Catania and the young singer, Giulia Mazzara, a Syracuse native, are already shuffling their feet. The wealthy British lords and ladies, for whom the concert is primarily being held, are already here, lightly mingled with local nobility and businesspeople from the area. Naturally the Monsignor must be here as well, a man still young and slim in his black robe, who worked until recently, someone whispers to me, in a very senior position at the Vatican, but wanted to return to his home city. Was there a transgression? Now we are asked to kindly take our places, on chairs prettily covered in yellow satin taffeta. The Baron gives a brief speech on the history of the house and the great ghosts we may still sense here: Admiral Horatio, naturally, and Emma and the kings of Naples and the venerable grand masters of the Order of Malta. Then the music starts. A great deal of Italian, Puccini, Mascagni, famous arias, including Vincenzo Bellini's 'Casta Diva', which Maria Callas sang so unforgettably. Giulia Mazzara acquits herself well. The wrinkled hearts of the elderly English fly to her.

Great applause. I too marvel at her voice, its fluent modulations and mastery across many registers. To conclude, a jaunty piece runs riot round the salon: the waltz from Dmitri Shostakovich's Jazz Suite No. 2. Everyone stands for the final applause. The atmosphere is good, the musicians a little heated, the bars under siege. For half an hour, the Baron fulfils his duties as host with a certain nonchalance and much chat, then takes me to one side.

'I'd like to show you the archive, where I keep my manuscript collection and all the documents connected to the history of the palace and my family.' He leads me to a gallery next to the private chapel. At the top of a spiral staircase, an emporium painted in radiant white sits in splendour, its multitude of drawers each sporting a Roman numeral and filled to the brim with tied and sealed bundles of parchment.

'Here lie treasures,' says Pietro and adds that he hopes he may still rescue a few more before he grows too old. He says this not wistfully but belligerently, and with a roguish twinkle in his eyes.

'Now is not the time to unwrap things. We'll do that on another occasion. Come on, let's sit outside on the balcony. In summer, this is the best spot in the Palazzo.'

He leads me onto the largest of the three balconies, the central one, which has a fabulous view over the whole of Piazza Duomo. There are some chairs already set out. A servant in dark-red livery arrives, bringing glasses and wine.

'I'd like to talk to you about a book project, which is very important to me. My family has always had good relations with the grand masters of the Order of Malta. I'm a member of the Order. I took part in the most recent General Chapter. It was fun. Thoroughly world-wise, decent gentlemen. But why am I telling you this? In my archive there are documents that cast a new light on Caravaggio, on his imprisonment on Malta, on the things the Order accused him of. Also, clues about his escape from jail, which was the maximum-security facility of its day, and his journey across to Syracuse. It's new, fresh material. Only I know about it. I'd like to write a book about it, to refute Bellori too, who is superficial and occasionally absurd.'

Now the Baroness arrives. She has said farewell to the last guests and seems, in spite of her seventy years, full of dynamism.

'Has my husband been ambushing you with his plans again? Plans which, alas, alas, alas, he will never put into action.' Yes, she says the word 'alas' three times, her eyebrows raised.

'You must write this book,' I say to the Baron. 'We're waiting for it.' I say this with all my emphasis, because in that moment, I believe it myself.

We talk further about his family, about the high costs that come with such a palace, about his yacht, which he wants to show me *la prossima volta*, as well as a few choice items from his archive.

Pietro has been portrayed to me as closed off and unapproachable. Suspicious even. I notice nothing of the kind tonight. Here is a man who has been able to preserve an inner realm, beyond all the ineffable obligations his status entails. He loves this palace; he burns for the history of Ortigia and for the history of his family.

It is already late as I say my farewells. '*Mille grazie*,' I shout to the two of them and '*Ci vediamo*' – See you soon! The cathedral square is empty, emptier than I've ever seen it. Only one or two shadowy figures flit past. I turn around one more time. In the Palazzo the lights are going out. As I step out of the cones of light on Piazza Minerva and turn into the darkness of Via Logoteta, the stars suddenly reveal themselves in the black sky. They hiss at me like fat poems and make my teeth crackle with happiness.

Acknowledgements

A profound thank you to all the friends who have helped me with tips and advice. To Etta Scollo above all, the person who first ignited my passion for Sicily. My heartfelt thanks also to Baron Pietro Beneventano del Bosco and Baron Lucio Tasca di Lignari for their hospitality, Dora Suma for her great helpfulness, and Andreas Rossmann for his knowledge of Sicily, shared so generously.

Some of the figures in this book, though they have factual, entirely real 'foundations', have been developed in fictional directions. I beg their indulgence, in the hope that they will accept this as a bonus.

June 2020–September 2022
Syracuse and Berlin

Bibliography

Alajmo, Roberto, *Palermo*, translated from the Italian by
Guido Waldman (London, 2010).

Baedekers Mittelmeer. Seewege, Hafenplätze, Landausflüge
(Leipzig, 1934).

Bellori, Giovanni Pietro, 'The Life of Michelangelo da
Caravaggio' in Helen Langdon and Howard Hibbard,
Lives of Caravaggio (London, 2016).

Brydone, Patrick and Beckford, William, *A Tour through
Sicily and Malta in a series of letters to William Beckford*
(London, 1775).

Bumm, Peter, *August Graf von Platen. Eine Biographie*
(Paderborn / Munich / Vienna, 1990).

Cibulka, Hanns, *Nachtwache. Tagebuch aus dem Kriege.
Sizilien 1943* (Halle / Leipzig, 1989).

Cicero, *The Verrine Orations*, translated from the Latin by
L. H. G. Greenwood (London, 1953).

Consolo, Vincenzo, *Le Pietre di Pantalica* (Milan, 1988).

Consolo, Vincenzo, *L'olivo e l'olivastro* (Milan, 1994).

Cronin, Vincent, *The Golden Honeycomb* (London, 1954).

Delius, Friedrich Christian, *Der Spaziergang von Rostock
nach Syrakus* (Hamburg, 1995).

Di Lampedusa, Giuseppe Tomasi, *The Leopard*, translated
from the Italian by Archibald Colquhoun (London,
1960).

Di Silvestro, Pino, *August von Platen* (Palermo, 1987).

Dummett, Jeremy, *Syracuse, City of Legends* (London, 2010).

Durrell, Lawrence, *Sicilian Carousel* (London, 1977).

Edwards, Andrew and Edwards, Suzanne (eds.), *Sicily: A Literary Guide for Travellers* (London, 2014).

Fest, Joachim, *Im Gegenlicht. Eine italienische Reise* (Berlin, 1988).

Gregorovius, Ferdinand, *Wanderjahre in Italien* (Munich, 1967).

Guzzetta, Giuseppe, *Le Collezioni Numismatiche del Museo di Siracusa* (Catania, 2012).

Jünger, Ernst, *Ein Inselfrühling* (Tübingen, 1949).

König, René, *Sizilien. Ein Buch von Städten und Höhlen, von Fels und Lava und von der großen Freiheit des Vulkans* (Zürich, 1943).

Lewis, Norman, *In Sicily* (London, 2000).

Norcia, Giuseppina, *Syracuse: A Sentimental Dictionary of the City* (Syracuse, 2016).

Norwich, John Julius, *Sicily* (London, 2015).

Ortheil, Hanns-Josef, *Die Insel der Dolci. In den süssen Paradiesen Siziliens*, with photos by Lotta Ortheil (Stuttgart, 2013).

Osterkamp, Ernst (ed.), *Sizilien. Reisebilder aus drei Jahrhunderten* (Munich, 1986).

Ovid, *The Metamorphoses*, translated from the Latin by A. D. Melville (Oxford, 1987).

Pindar, *The Complete Odes*, translated from the Ancient Greek by Anthony Verity (Oxford, 2007).

Pasolini, Pier Paolo, *The Long Road of Sand*, translated from the Italian by Stephen Sartarelli (Rome, 2015).

Robb, Peter, *Midnight in Sicily* (London, 1998).

Rossmann, Andreas, *Mit dem Rücken zum Meer. Ein sizilianisches Tagebuch*, with photos by Barbara Klemm (Cologne, 2017).

Russell, George, *A Tour through Sicily in the Year 1815* (London, 1819).

Scandaliato, Angela and Mulè, Nucio, *Jewish Itineraries in Syracuse: The Synagogue and the Ritual Baths* (Florence, 2017).

Scianna, Ferdinando, *Autoritratto di un fotografo* (Rome, 2021).

Sciascia, Leonardo, *Mein Sizilien*, translated from the Italian by Martina Kempter and Sigrid Vagt (Berlin, 1995).

Sciascia, Leonardo, *Nero su Nero* (Turin, 1980).

Sciascia, Leonardo, *The Wine-Dark Sea*, translated from the Italian by Avril Bardoni (London, 2014).

Scollo, Etta, *Voci di Sicilia. Eine Reise durch Sizilien*, edited and translated into German from the Italian by Klaudia Ruschkowski (Wiesbaden, 2020).

Seferis, George, *Collected Poems*, revised edition, edited and translated from the Greek by Edmund Keeley and Philip Sherrard (Princeton, 1995).

Seume, Johann Gottfried, *A Stroll to Syracuse*, translated from the German by Alexander and Elizabeth Henderson (London, 1964).

Virgil, *The Aeneid*, translated from the Latin by Robert Fagles (London, 2006).

Vittorini, Elio, *The Red Carnation*, translated from the Italian by Anthony Bower (London, 1953).

Vittorini, Elio, *Conversations in Sicily*, translated from the Italian by Alane Salierno Mason (New York, 2000).